D0629954

THE
JANE AUSTEN
POCKET BIBLE

THE
JANE AUSTEN
POCKET BIBLE

HOLLY IVINS

This edition first published in Great Britain 2010 by
Crimson Publishing, a division of Crimson Business Ltd
Westminster House
Kew Road
Richmond
Surrey
TW9 2ND

A catalogue record for this book is available from the British Library.

ISBN 978 1907087 09 7

Printed and bound by L.E.G.O. S.p.A, Lavis (TN)

ACKNOWLEDGEMENTS

A big thank you to Sally, Beth, all the lovely Crimsonettes, and everyone at Crimson Publishing. Huge thanks go to Jack who boasted as much about this book as Henry Austen did about *Pride and Prejudice*.

I couldn't have done this without my Mom, who is always my biggest fan; and Andrew, who is my fantastic editor, motivator and my very own Mr Knightley.

CONTENTS

INTRODUCTION

'I declare after all there is no enjoyment like reading! How much sooner one tires of anything than of a book!' Pride and Prejudice (1813)

'It is a truth universally acknowledged . . .' that Jane Austen is one of the most beloved novelists in the English language. Her novels have never been out of print since their publication in the 19th century and there have been innumerable adaptations of her novels in both film and television. That doesn't make her novels any less intimidating to approach for the first time reader though, or even for the avowed fan to get to grips with the finer details.

This book is here to help. For those who have never entered the world of Miss Austen, this book will be a guide to help navigate through the ironic turn of phrase, the love triangles and the bonnets. For those self-confessed 'Janeites', there are fun facts about the novels as well as a different look at the love and romance found within the pages of the novels. This book will help you learn more about the lady herself, her life, and the world she lived in: all adding to your understanding of these great works of fiction.

By the end of this Pocket Bible you should be able to approach these novels as old friends, not intimidating classical tomes. You should be able to read these beloved classics and understand the intriguing storylines as well as the social commentary and the delightful literary art which Austen employs.

'Life seems but a quick succession of busy nothings': Biography

You may already know everything there is to know about Mr Darcy, Emma Woodhouse and Catherine Morland, or you may still be trying to figure out which Bennet sister is which, but how much do you know about the woman who created these memorable characters? This chapter is a brief look at Jane's life, including details on how she wrote her novels, in the hope that by becoming better acquainted with the author, you will become better acquainted with her work.

☙ TIMELINE OF JANE ❧ AUSTEN'S LIFE

BIRTH AND CHILDHOOD (1775–1801)

Jane Austen was born on December 16 1775 at the Steventon rectory in Hampshire, a county in the south of England; She was the seventh child for the Austen family, followed only by her brother Charles. She had six brothers and one sister, Cassandra, whom she was extremely close to (see p. 2 for more on Jane's family). Jane's father was the reverend at Steventon rectory and her mother, an intelligent and sensible woman, ran the household, caring for her own children as well as the boys who boarded at their house and were educated by Mr Austen.

After her christening on April 5 1776 Jane was sent to live with and be nursed by a nearby farmer's wife, Elizabeth Littlewood. Although this may seem cruel, it was exactly the same treatment as her siblings had experienced in their infancy. Mrs Austen simply didn't have time to look after five boys and an infant as well as running her household. Jane's family often visited her though, and the young Austen returned to live with them when she was about two or three years old.

Jane spent a happy childhood at Steventon, full of reading and long country walks. She was apparently a tomboy as a child, preferring to play cricket and roll down hills with her brothers rather than play 'girls' games', much like the character of Catherine Morland in *Northanger Abbey*. The Austen house was a full one with eight children, and an additional four or five boys who lived there to be educated by Jane's father.

Pocket Fact 🔱

Jane's brother Henry remembered that Jane began reading at a very young age and that she had a 'tenacious memory'.

The Austen family

Father: Reverend George Austen (1731–1805)
Jane's father won a scholarship to St John's College at Oxford University and while there he was known as 'The Handsome Proctor'. George greatly encouraged Jane's writing, buying her her first notebooks to write in, and even approaching a publisher for her with her early draft of *Pride and Prejudice*.

Mother: Cassandra Austen (née Leigh) (1739–1827)
Cassandra Leigh's uncle was a master (ie the principal) at Balliol College at Oxford University and it was while visiting this uncle that Cassandra met George Austen. They were married in 1764 and Cassandra went on to have eight children, run a household, care for the school boys who boarded in the house, and even write poetry.

Siblings: James Austen (1765–1819)
James was the eldest son of the Austen family, and became rector of Steventon after his father retired. James' children Anne and James-Edward are responsible for most of the biographical information we have about Jane.

George Austen (1766–1838)

George was named after his father but he did not live with the Austens as he suffered from epilepsy, living instead with neighbors in Steventon. There is evidence to suggest George may have been deaf as Jane makes reference to the fact that she was fluent in 'finger speaking'. Not a lot of information has survived about George, and he and Jane are the only members of the Austen family who did not have an official portrait taken.

Edward Austen (1767–1852)

As a child Edward was adopted by Thomas Knight, Mr Austen's wealthy cousin, and after taking the surname Knight went on to inherit several estates, including Godmersham an estate in the county of Kent in south-east England.

Henry Austen (1771–1850)

Henry was Jane's favorite brother, often acting as her representative with publishers in London. Henry enjoyed a varied career as an army agent in the militia, a banker, and eventually as a country curate (a type of minister). He married the Austens' cousin Eliza de Feuillide and they lived together in London. It was Henry who prepared *Northanger Abbey* and *Persuasion* for publication after Jane's death.

Cassandra Elizabeth Austen (1773–1845)

Cassandra was Jane's best friend and the sisters lived together for the entirety of Jane's life. Their mother even said 'if Cassandra's head had been going to be cut off, Jane would have hers cut off too'. When Jane died Cassandra said 'She was the sun of my life, the gilder of every pleasure, the soother of every sorrow. I had not a thought concealed from her, and it is as if I had lost part of myself.' In the brief periods they were apart the sisters wrote to each other frequently and there are about 100 surviving letters. There are no letters from Jane before the age of 20 though as Cassandra destroyed the majority of her sister's letters after Jane's death. Although Cassandra destroyed most of Jane's letters she is responsible for passing on her sister's legacy to her nephews and nieces, and also produced the only two portraits we have of Jane.

> ## Jane's letters
> *If you want to get a sense of what Jane Austen was really like, try reading her letters. There are several collections available and they all give a brilliant insight into the author's scathing wit and ironic view of the world.*

Francis Austen (1774–1865)

Francis was known affectionately as Frank or 'Fly' by his family and at the age of 12 he went to Portsmouth to join the Naval Academy. He went on to become the Admiral of the Fleet in 1863 and even received a knighthood. It was Frank's second wife Martha who wrote *The Jane Austen Household Book*.

Charles Austen (1779–1852)

Charles was the youngest in the Austen family and also joined the navy at age 12. He was made an Admiral in 1846 and gave Jane a topaz cross, a gesture Jane inserted into *Mansfield Park* when William gives Fanny a cross when he returns from sea.

Reading in the Austen household

The Austens were a family of great readers and Jane started writing at the age of 12. The work she produced in this period (between the ages of 12 and 18) is referred to as her *Juvenilia* (see p. 65 for more on this). Jane's early motivation was to write short pieces of fiction as gifts for her family and she would often read her work aloud to her family in the evenings. Cassandra recalled Jane reading *Elinor and Marianne* to the family before 1796 as well as an early draft of *Pride and Prejudice*, both of which were 'established favorites'. The Austen household has been described as one full of intellectual discussion and Jane's father encouraged her writing and guided her in her reading.

Pocket Fact 🕴

Mr Austen's bookcase covered 64 square feet of wall in the Steventon rectory, full of both classical works and new novels.

Jane's education

Jane's formal education began at boarding school with her sister. The girls went to Mrs Cawley's school in Oxford when Jane was aged seven. This turned out to be a disaster, as an outbreak of typhus nearly killed both girls. Luckily their parents brought them home and nursed them back to health. Later in 1785, the 10-year-old Jane was sent to the Abbey School in Reading, in Berkshire, about 13 miles from her home in Steventon (or rather she insisted on going with Cassandra). This school was run by Madame la Tournelle, a kind woman who taught the girls sewing and spelling. Jane was happy during her time here, and Mrs Goddard's boarding school in *Emma* seems to have been based on the Abbey School.

Pocket Fact 🕴

Jane was not the only writer in the Austen family. Her mother wrote many poems during her lifetime, and also wrote some scathing accounts of their neighbors, a sarcastic wit she clearly passed on to Jane. James Austen produced a magazine called The Loiterer *which was published in London, Birmingham, Bath, Reading and Oxford. Henry Austen also contributed articles to this magazine.*

Jane's social life

At home, Jane put on plays with her brothers and sister, much as the Bertram family do in *Mansfield Park*. The family normally preferred comedies such as Sheridan's *The Rivals* but in 1788 they staged a more elaborate production with the help of Jane's sophisticated older cousin Eliza de Feuillide (see p. 17).

Jane enjoyed a full social life at Steventon, attending dances at the Assembly Rooms in the nearby town of Basingstoke, as well as attending private balls at Manydown, the large country estate of family friends, the Biggs. Jane also enjoyed trips to London during this time, to visit her brother Henry.

Pocket Fact ⚜

The Assembly Rooms in Basingstoke where Jane attended dances is now a Barclays bank, bearing a plaque stating that Jane danced there.

It was during this time that Jane met Tom Lefroy, one of the men she is thought to have been romantically involved with. See Chapter 7 for more on Jane's own romantic adventures.

In 1800 Jane's father, now aged 70, decided to retire. When he announced this news, along with the revelation that they would have to leave the rectory and move to Bath, it is said that Jane fainted.

What she wrote during this time

Between 1787 and 1793 Jane worked on what is now known as her *Juvenilia*. She spent a great deal of time revising these works and copied 29 different works into three notebooks. These notebooks included *Love and Freindship* [sic] a satire of the sensibility novels which were popular at the time. She also penned her version of *The History of England*, a 34 page manuscript illustrated with watercolors by Cassandra. This history was another satire, this time parodying the historical writing popular at the time, such as *The History of England* by Oliver Goldsmith. In 1793 Jane began work on a play called *Sir Charles Grandison*, which she temporarily abandoned but finished in 1800.

Pocket Fact ⚜

Some of Jane's earliest encouragement for her writing came from her neighbor Anne Lefroy, or Madame Lefroy as she was known. Anne was a lively and intelligent woman who was a great reader of Milton, Pope and Shakespeare, and was even known to write poetry herself. Incidentally, Madame Lefroy was also the aunt of Tom Lefroy, Jane's childhood sweetheart.

At this time (1795–1799) Jane also began work on early versions of her novels: *Elinor and Marianne* would later become *Sense and Sensibility*, *First Impressions* was the foundation of *Pride and Prejudice* and *Susan* was an early draft of *Northanger Abbey*. Between 1793 and 1795 Jane worked on her most ambitious work up to that point, *Lady Susan*, which she completed in 1803. This work differs greatly from Jane's other writing, depicting an older heroine, a sexual predator, who uses her intelligence and charm to manipulate those around her (see p. 71 for more on this novel).

In 1797 Jane's father approached a publisher in London, Thomas Cadell, to see if he would consider publishing *First Impressions*, which George Austen described as 'a Manuscript Novel, comprised in three Vols. about the length of Miss Burney's *Evelina*'. The letter was returned though, marked 'declined by return of post'. Jane then returned to working on *Elinor and Marianne* from 1797 to 1798, removing the letter format and drafting it into the more familiar *Sense and Sensibility*.

In 1789 it is believed that Jane decided to try and write professionally, although in his autobiographical notice Jane's brother Henry was careful to point out that 'she became an authoress entirely from taste and inclination. Neither the hope of fame nor profit mixed with her early motives.' However, this statement seems to have been born out of the building of the myth of 'Saint Jane', which the author's family perpetuated after her death. Jane in fact was very conscious of the commercial success of her books, and was always aware of her profits and copyright earnings, as a letter to her brother Frank discussing her earnings from *Sense and Sensibility* shows: 'I have now therefore written myself into £250 – which only makes me long for more' (about $22,000 now).

BATH (1801–1806)

In 1801 Jane, Cassandra and their parents arrived in Bath, in the county of Somerset in south-west England, (her brothers had all left home by this time). Although Jane preferred her quiet country life in Steventon she did have an active social life in Bath.

While living in Bath the family would go on trips to the beach in Dorset and Lyme Regis. It was while in Lyme Regis that Jane is said to have had a mysterious romantic encounter with a young man who was very taken with her, but who tragically died before their relationship could develop. It was also during this period of her life in 1802 that Jane received her only proposal of marriage. (For more on Jane's love life see Chapter 7).

In 1805 Jane's father died suddenly after a short illness. This left Jane, her mother and Cassandra in a precarious financial situation. The women now had only a very small allowance which had to be supplemented by Jane's brothers, coming to a total of only £450 a year (a combined household income comparable to about $22,950 now). Considering that in 1807 Jane's budget for the entire year was just £50 (from which she had to buy clothes, send letters, and entertain herself among other things) it is easy to see that this money didn't go very far to support three women with no other means of income. The women remained in rented accommodation in Bath, and were joined by Jane's sister-in-law Martha in 1805.

What she wrote during this time

Jane did very little writing during her time in Bath. She managed to sell her manuscript *Susan* (now called *Northanger Abbey*) to a publisher for £10 (about $510 now) but the book was never published. Jane also began work on a novel called *The Watsons* (see p. 92) but soon abandoned it after the death of her father.

Some people have argued that while she was living in Bath Jane was too depressed to write; others that she was simply too busy. Whatever the reason this period was certainly the least productive for Jane's writing.

SOUTHAMPTON AND GODMERSHAM (1805–1808)

The period between 1805 and 1808 was a tumultuous time for Jane as she, her mother and sister moved between family members, staying where they could. In 1806 some relief from this nomadic lifestyle came when Jane's brother Frank invited the women to come and live with him and his new wife in Southampton on the south coast of England. Jane was pleased to leave Bath and Southampton also had the added advantage of being near Portsmouth, where Jane's brothers Frank and Charles were stationed in their naval careers.

What she wrote during this time

Due to her frequent moves and unsettled lifestyle this was another unproductive period for Jane. In 1809 she tried to buy back her manuscript for *Susan* from the publisher, but couldn't afford to pay the £10 they asked for.

CHAWTON (1808–1817)

In 1808 Edward Austen's wife Elizabeth sadly died during the birth of her 11th child. Edward then invited his mother and sisters to live at a cottage in the grounds of his Chawton estate in Hampshire. The six bedroom cottage was close to Steventon, where Jane's brother James was now the rector, and the women happily moved into the cottage. The family led a quiet, private life and while she lived at Chawton Jane spent her time in much the same way every day: she would wake up, practise the pianoforte (the traditional term for a piano, see glossary), cook breakfast for the household and then go and work on her writing, having fulfilled her household duties for the day.

What she wrote during this time

Jane's thirties proved to be the most productive period of her life, as she published four novels, completed one, and began another. Between 1808 and 1811 Jane reworked both *Elinor and Marianne* and *First Impressions*, changing their titles to the now familiar *Sense and Sensibility* and *Pride and Prejudice*. *Sense and Sensibility* was published in 1811 and *Pride and Prejudice* was published in 1813 by Thomas Egerton (for more on these novels see Chapter 5). Jane then moved to the publisher John Murray and wrote *Mansfield Park*, which was published in 1814 (p. 71), followed by *Emma* in 1815 (p. 75). *Mansfield Park* was ignored by reviewers but proved very popular nonetheless, selling out in six months and requiring a second edition in 1815. This second edition exhausted demand, however, and the failure was only offset by the success of *Emma*.

What did Jane Austen look like?

There are only two verified portraits of Jane Austen – both done by her sister Cassandra. One is a view of Jane's back and the other was said by her niece Anna to be 'hideously unlike' Jane. There seems to have been some disagreement within her family over Jane's looks, with her aunt Phila saying she was, 'not at all pretty' while others remembered her as 'fair and handsome', and others still that she had 'a clear brown complexion, darkish brown hair and hazel eyes'. Most accounts of Jane make mention of her eyes though, suggesting they were her best feature.

The Jane Austen Center in Bath commissioned a portrait artist to create a more accurate portrait of Jane, using Cassandra's portrait and FBI forensic techniques, altering it to match the portraits of the other Austen family members, along with the written accounts of Jane's appearance. The image is very different to Cassandra's portrait so we are only left to guess about what Jane really looked like.

LIFE AS A PUBLISHED AUTHOR

Jane's novels were all published anonymously by 'A Lady' and only Jane's family knew her identity as the author. This proved to be a great family joke, and there is one account of Jane's niece Anna, while in a library with Jane and Cassandra, picking up a copy of *Sense and Sensibility* and saying 'Oh that must be rubbish, I am sure from the title', much to her aunts' amusement. In 1813 after *Pride and Prejudice* had published to favorable reviews and was widely popular, Henry let Jane's identity as the author slip when he couldn't help telling someone who was praising *Pride and Prejudice* that the author was his sister.

Pocket Fact 𝕎

Writing was considered to be a scandalous occupation for a woman at this time. Most women preserved their reputation by publishing anonymously and one contemporary of Jane's, Mary Brunton, in explaining why she would never allow her name to be known said: 'To be pointed at – to be noticed & commented upon – to be suspected of literary airs – to be shunned, as literary women are . . . My dear, I would sooner exhibit myself as a rope dancer'.

Henry often acted as a representative for his sister at her publishers in London and she often stayed with him when correcting proofs of her novels. In 1813 Henry fell ill and was attended by the Prince Regent's physician. This connection allowed Jane to learn that the Prince Regent, George IV, was a big fan of her work and that he kept a set of her novels at all of his residences. Jane was introduced to the Prince's librarian, Mr Clarke, who invited her (or rather ordered her) to dedicate her latest novel, *Emma*, to the Prince. A few years later Jane wrote a satirical piece called 'Plan of a novel', which is thought to have been based on the suggestions Mr Clarke made for her next novel.

Falling ill

Emma (1815) was Jane's last novel to be published in her lifetime. She had begun work on a new novel called *The Elliots* (later published as *Persuasion*) in 1816 and in the same year Henry had bought back the manuscript and copyright of her novel *Susan* from the publisher who had acquired it 14 years earlier. Jane was forced to postpone publishing these novels though, as her family met with further financial difficulty. The bank where her brother Henry worked – and where her other brothers had invested their money – failed, leaving Henry deeply in debt and losing all of the Austen brothers large sums of money. Things were so dire for Henry and Frank that they were unable to continue financially supporting their mother and sisters.

During this black period, Jane began to feel unwell. Struggling on, she decided to change the ending of *The Elliots* and finally completed it in 1817. She began work on another novel called *The Brothers* (later called *Sanditon*) but soon became too weak to continue. She had to begin writing with a pencil rather than a quill pen but by March 1817 she had to stop writing entirely.

WINCHESTER (1817)

In March 1817 Jane became so weak that she was forced to stop writing, and in April that year she penned her will. By May her condition had deteriorated so much that she moved to Winchester in Hampshire to be nearer her doctor. Jane died peacefully on July 18 1817 with her head in Cassandra's lap. There have been many theories put forward to explain her death, including Addison's disease, Hodgkin's lymphoma and bovine tuberculosis, although the exact cause remains obscure.

Through her family's clerical connections it was arranged that Jane would be laid to rest in Winchester Cathedral, where she was buried on 24 July 1817.

The epitaph on Jane's grave reads:

'In Memory of JANE AUSTEN, youngest daughter of the late Revd GEORGE AUSTEN, formerly Rector of Steventon in this County. She departed this Life on the 18th of July 1817, aged 41, after a long illness supported with the patience and the hopes of a Christian. The benevolence of her heart, the sweetness of her temper, and the extraordinary endowments of her mind obtained the regard of all who knew her and the warmest love of her intimate connections. Their grief is in proportion to their affection, they know their loss to be irreparable, but in their deepest affliction they are consoled by a firm though humble hope that her charity, devotion, faith and purity have rendered her soul acceptable in the sight of her REDEEMER.'

While this inscription mentions the 'extraordinary endowments of her mind' it does not mention the fact that Jane was a writer. However, an obituary of Jane appeared in *The Gentleman's Magazine* in 1817, reading, 'At Winchester, Miss Jane Austen, youngest daughter of Rev. George Austen, Rector of Steventon, Hants, authoress of *Emma*, *Mansfield Park*, *Pride and Prejudice* and *Sense and Sensibility*.'

In 1872 another plaque was added by Jane's nephew James Edward Austen-Leigh and in 1900 public funds paid for the installation of a stained glass window depicting St Augustine, with a Latin inscription which reads, 'Remember in the Lord Jane Austen, who died 18 July, AD 1817.'

Pocket Fact 💧

On making out her will Jane Austen noted how much profit she had made from her novels. The amount came to £84 and 13 shillings (about $4,300 now).

Publishing Jane's last two novels

Later in 1817 Henry published *Persuasion* and *Northanger Abbey* as a combined edition. It is likely that Henry changed the titles of these novels from the working titles of *The Elliots* and *Susan* which Jane had used. These two novels represented Jane's first and final completed works. While the name of the author is still not given on the volume, Henry included a biographical notice of the author in the publication, which openly identified Jane as the author of her novels for the first time in any of her published works.

Pocket Fact 💧

Many readers have often wondered if Jane's characters were based on real people: was there a real Mr Darcy or Elizabeth Bennet? Jane's family were always quick to defend her saying that she wanted to 'create not reproduce' and that she was too proud of her 'gentlemen to admit that they were only Mr A or Colonel B'.

AFTER JANE'S DEATH

After Jane's death, Cassandra made sure that her nephews and nieces knew all about their aunt, regaling them with stories about her life and her writing. Unfortunately she also drastically reduced sources for future biographers by burning something like 3,500 letters that she had received from Jane. Jane also kept no diary – another hindrance for biographers searching for clues about the real Jane Austen – but she did keep careful notes about her novels and made lists of the comments her novels received from friends and family. As a result of this most of the information we have about Jane's life comes from family accounts written almost 50 years after her death.

MEMOIRS

The first memoir of Jane that appeared was the biographical notice which Henry included in the combined edition of *Northanger Abbey* and *Persuasion*. In it he describes Jane's life as 'A life of usefulness, literature, and religion [which] was not by any means a life of event.' The next biography of Jane was written by her nephew James Edward Austen-Leigh, whose *Memoir of Jane Austen* appeared in December 1869. He also described Jane's life as a quiet one, saying it was 'singularly barren of events'. The picture painted of Jane by these Victorian era familial accounts is of a 'Saint Jane' who was a good Christian and devoted family member. At times, however, this image of a perfect Jane can seem slightly at odds with the sarcasm and scathing wit found in her letters and novels.

Pocket Fact 🕎

In 1894 George Saintsbury coined the term 'Janeite' to describe Austen fans. The term didn't become widely popular though until 1924 when Rudyard Kipling used the word in one of his short stories.

🐚 HOW JANE WROTE 🐚

Not only did Jane produce some of the most memorable stories in literature, the stories of how she wrote her novels are themselves worthy of retelling.

While at Steventon, as Jane's brothers gradually left home over the years, she and Cassandra eventually inherited a room next to their bedroom. It was in the privacy of this room that Jane wrote her *Juvenilia*, as well as the early drafts of *Sense and Sensibility*, *Pride and Prejudice* and *Northanger Abbey*.

Pocket Fact 🕎

In 1794 Jane's father bought her a mahogany writing desk. This 'desk' was actually a sloped box which could be used to write on and to keep papers, quills and so on inside. There was also a glass ink stand. The desk was portable, allowing Jane to take her writing with her and carry on in any location. The desk is now in the British Library in London, on display in the Treasures Room.

When Jane, her mother and her sister moved to the cottage at Chawton she didn't have the luxury of a private study and her nephew James Edward, in his memoir of Jane, relates how guarded she was about her work. Jane was forced to work in the sitting room which was used by the whole household, meaning she was often interrupted. Jane apparently used very small pieces of paper which she could easily hide during one of these interruptions. Jane was also given warning of interruptions by the now infamous 'creaking door'. James recounts that a door on the approach to the sitting room creaked when it was opened. Jane refused to let the door be repaired so she could be sure of an early warning of some-one's approach to be able to hide her work.

It is also said that Jane would never sit on the couch in this room (which was her mother's seat) and instead would use two chairs to fashion a kind of sofa for herself. She claimed she was comfortable on this contrived seat but it doesn't sound like the best place to write! When one thinks of how many works Jane produced during this time (revising *Sense and Sensibility*, *Pride and Prejudice* and completing *Mansfield Park*, *Emma* and *Persuasion*) it is hard not to be impressed by her methods and dedication to her work in spite of less than ideal conditions.

Pocket Fact ♟

If you want to become a true 'Janeite' why not join one of the many Jane Austen societies which have been set up all over the world? The Jane Austen Society of North America has over 60 regional groups and organizes lectures, dances and even produces journals for its members. There are also Jane Austen societies in Great Britain, Australia and Buenos Aires.

2

'If things are going untowardly one month, they are sure to mend the next': History and context

This chapter will look at the major historical events which occurred during Jane's lifetime, as well as giving a brief explanation of the society she lived in. By understanding the context of the world Jane was writing in we can more vividly understand the world she creates in her novels.

☙ HISTORY OF JANE'S LIFETIME: ☙ TIMELINE OF MAJOR EVENTS (1775–1817)

- 1776: Signing of the American Declaration of Independence

- 1779: British Penitentiary Acts mark the introduction of state prisons in Britain

- 1783: Evacuation of British troops and those loyal to the crown from American colonies

- 1783: William Pitt the Younger becomes Prime Minister of Great Britain and the Treaty of Paris ends the American Revolution

- 1787: Convicts are sent to Australia from Britain for the first time

- 1787: Formation of the Committee for the Abolition of the Slave Trade in Britain

- 1788: Regency crisis after George III's first attack of madness

● 1789: Storming of the Bastille: The French Revolution

On July 14 1789 a mob stormed the Bastille prison in Paris, marking the beginning of the French Revolution. The revolt began over the financial state of France and the extreme under-representation of the lower classes, which left common people starving and the aristocrats living a life of decadent luxury. In 1792 the National Convention abolished the monarchy and declared France a republic. In 1793 Louis XVI was executed for treason.

Between 1793 and 1794 the Jacobin leader Robespierre ordered a number of guillotine executions, causing the period to be dubbed 'the Reign of Terror'. Then in 1794 Robespierre himself was executed. Meanwhile the French armies were gathering power and in 1799 a young general called Napoleon led a coup in Paris and named himself the first consul, the leader of France. This marked the end of the Revolution and the beginning of military rule in France.

Pocket Fact 👑

Jane's closest connection to the French Revolution was her intriguing cousin Eliza de Feuillide. Eliza was born Elizabeth Hancock in India, and she was educated in London and France. She married a French officer Jean Capot de Feuillide, making her Comtesse de Feuillide, but her husband was guillotined in 1794. Eliza visited the Austens in 1787 when she was 25 and Jane was aged 11. Jane must have been very impressed by her glamorous French cousin, and Eliza is thought to have inspired Love and Freindship [sic], Lady Susan *and the character of Mary Crawford in* Mansfield Park.

What did this mean for Jane?

England was a place of paranoia and fear during the French Revolution as the aristocrats nervously watched the growth of the revolutionary ideas being espoused in France, especially after the revolution which had just taken place in America which ended British rule there. Jane was most closely affected by the Revolution when her cousin Eliza's husband was guillotined during the Reign of Terror (see above).

In Her Own Words 🜚

'History, real solemn history, I cannot be interested in . . . I read it a little as a duty; but it tells me nothing that does not either vex or weary me. The quarrels of popes and kings, with wars and pestilences in every page; the men all so good for nothing, and hardly any women at all — it is very tiresome.'

Catherine Morland, Northanger Abbey

- **1793: Britain goes to war with France**

The execution of Louis XVI seemingly justified Britain's growing fear of France and proved the catalyst for war with the French Republic. France had been fighting battles with other European powers since 1792 but it wasn't until this execution that the British government was spurred into action and joined the anti-French coalition. Although the Treaty of Amiens was signed in 1802, Napoleon used this time of supposed peace to rebuild his armies and declare war again in 1803. Napoleon declared himself Emperor of France in 1804 and seemed to genuinely plan on taking over the world. In 1805 Britain displayed her naval prowess by defeating Napoleon at the Battle of Trafalgar but Napoleon continued to conquer mainland Europe until 1815 when he was finally defeated at the Battle of Waterloo.

What did this mean for Jane?

The proximity of France and England meant that there was a constant fear of invasion during the time of Napoleon's rise and it gave rise to the formation of the militia regiments, just like those that appear in Jane's novels. Jane's brother Henry was a part of the Oxford militia from 1793 until 1800. Jane was most directly affected by the Napoleonic war through her brothers' involvement with the navy: Frank and Charles both served during this time, although Frank missed the Battle of Trafalgar as his ship was in Malta. Jane's novels show the utmost respect for the navy, particularly *Persuasion*, which praises the navy's fraternal spirit amongst its officers.

Pocket Fact 🔱

Jane was proud of her brothers' naval careers and made sure to be factually accurate in her descriptions of naval life. She even used the names of Frank's ships in her novels.

- 1798: United Irishmen rebel against British rule
- 1801: The Act of Union creates the United Kingdom of Great Britain and Ireland
- 1805: Battle of Trafalgar
- 1807: Britain abolishes the slave trade
- **1812: George IV as Prince Regent**

In 1811 George III fell ill again, and following the precedent set in 1788, power was given to his son George IV without the king's consent. The Prince was known for his extravagant and decadent lifestyle – by 1824 his lavish diet meant that he had a 50 inch waist! The Regency period (as it became known) was noted for its extravagant fashions and the excessive lifestyle of the upper classes. It must be noted that Austen herself never engaged in the decadence of the period though. See p. 21 for more on Regency society.

- 1815: Battle of Waterloo

Pocket Fact 🔱

In 2009 Jane Austen was credited as a co-author of a new work, Pride and Prejudice and Zombies. *This novel, published by Quirk Books, uses most of Austen's original text but with the added twist that the country has been overrun by a zombie plague. The book has been incredibly successful and a prequel called* Pride and Prejudice and Zombies: The Dawn of the Dreadfuls *has also been published.*

🐚 FINDING CONTEXTUAL HISTORY 🐚 IN JANE'S WRITING

Jane Austen makes barely any mention of contemporary political events in her work. Although her novels are based in the society of her age, she only ever alludes to the issues of the day. While some have criticized her for this, others think that her writing offered a breath of fresh air from the overly political and moralized writing of the time, much the same as the fantasy, romance, Gothic and adventure novels which were hugely popular at the time. While Jane focuses on morals and behaviors, she focuses on those relevant at any time, and chooses to base her moral examinations in the home, a setting which was relevant to everyone. She differs from other writers of her day who suffered from the 'French disease' of preaching moral issues: instead she presents characters whose behavior and fates helps us decide for ourselves the best ways to act.

Pocket Fact 🔱

Jane's niece Caroline recalled the lack of political commentary in her aunt's work when she said, 'Anyone might naturally desire to know what part such a mind as her's had taken in the great strifes of war and policy which so disquieted Europe for more than 20 years . . . in vain do I try to recall any word or expression of Aunt Jane's that had reference to public events'.

There are some slight allusions to her contextual history in Jane's work though. See if you can spot:

- The slave trade in *Mansfield Park*
- The 1780 Gordon Riots in London in *Northanger Abbey*
- The militia presence in *Pride and Prejudice*
- The naval presence in *Persuasion*

🐚 SOCIETY AS JANE KNEW IT 🐚

English society during Jane's time (dubbed Regency society after the rule of the Prince Regent) was based firmly on a class hierarchy, meaning that people were treated and recognized in direct accordance with their wealth and social status. Social classes descended in prestige from the Royal family to the nobility, the gentry, the clergy and finally to the working class. Jane's family was part of the gentry, meaning her father was considered a gentleman. It is this class which populates Jane's novels although we are sometimes introduced to characters from other classes, such as the nobility (Lady Catherine or the Dowager Viscountess Dalrymple) or the clergy (Mr Collins and Mr Elton).

Most people knew their place in society and reverence or condescension to higher and lower classes was observed on a daily basis. For example, people from a lower class would never address a member of a higher class by his or her first name. Jane always praises those members of the gentry who behave well to those considered lower than them, and mocks those who behave badly. Compare the presentation and fates of Lady Catherine in *Pride and Prejudice* and Mr Knightley in *Emma* with regards to their treatment of the lower classes, for example.

Pocket Fact 🔱

In Emma, *Harriet Smith is Emma Woodhouse's best friend. But throughout the entire novel she never uses her name Emma, she always refers to her as Miss Woodhouse. This may seem odd but it is merely because Harriet is observing that Emma is her social superior.*

THE GENTRY

To be considered a part of the landed gentry, a family had to own at least 300 acres of property. A male member of this class was known as a 'gentleman' (although, confusingly, not everyone called a gentleman was part of the gentry). Jane's father was part of the gentry, but he was from the lower end of the class while

Jane's mother had been part of a much wealthier gentry family. All of Jane's heroines are members of the gentry and range from the lower end of the class (like Catherine Morland) to the higher end (like Emma Woodhouse).

Essential traits of the gentry included:

- Owning at least 300 acres of land

- A sizeable income from this land or from a career

- A good family name

- Correct behavior

It is important to remember when reading Jane's novels, that although some men are called 'gentlemen', such as Mr Bennet, they would not necessarily have the land and wealth which were essential to be a part of the gentry. The strict social nuances of gentry society can be the most difficult part of Austen's novels for modern readers to grasp. The trick is to remember that people would be expected to remember their social level, and would be expected to act according to this level. It is also worth bearing in mind though that it was during Austen's time that a change in social values was occurring which would change these attitudes forever.

TIMES OF CHANGE

Jane's lifetime spanned both the American and French revolutions. While there was no violent revolution in England, there was a noticeable shift in social classes, as those with newfound wealth began to surpass the traditional land-owning classes in power and influence. The landed gentry looked on nervously as those with new money made from business, or naval officers with large fortunes made from prize money, began to be recognized and treated as gentlemen, even though they didn't perhaps meet the traditional criteria.

Persuasion is a perfect example of Jane's portrayal of these class shifts. Jane puts the rising family, Captain Wentworth and the Crofts, in direct opposition to the fading gentry family, the Elliots. Not only are the Elliots forced to give up their inherited property due to their debts, but the family who take the property from them have none of the qualities that Sir Walter considers essential parts of a gentleman.

Jane makes reference to this shifting class dynamic in most of her novels, presenting these 'new money' characters in both positive and negative ways. For example, she is happy to be positive about hard working families such as the Coles in *Emma* who have made their fortune and have risen through the social ranks without forgetting their roots, but characters like Mrs Elton, who Jane makes fun of for her newly acquired airs and graces from her sister's fortunate marriage, are shown only in a negative light.

In Her Own Words ◉

The Musgrove family in Persuasion *can be taken as an example of this shift in class consciousness as the family is described in a way that highlights Jane's acknowledgement of the shift, but in a manner that also shows she has not decided if these changes are for the better:* 'The Musgroves, like their houses, were in a state of alteration, perhaps of improvement. Their father and mother were in the old English style and the young people in the new. Mr and Mrs Musgrove were a very good sort of people; friendly and hospitable, not much educated, and not at all elegant. Their children had more modern minds and manners.'

🐚 HOW TO BEHAVE IN REGENCY 🐚 SOCIETY

Manners were of the utmost importance in Regency society; they were one of the most important displays of a person's class and wealth. Regency manners were loosely based on ideas from Renaissance Italy and on ideas and fashions from 17th century France, although the conduct guides of the time updated these ideas and made them more period specific.

One of the most important modes of behavior in Regency society was knowing your place. It was of the utmost importance that a person acted according to his or her station in life. A person's rank in society dictated the order in which they should enter a room, whom they could or could not speak to, and with whom it was appropriate to be on friendly terms with.

A person's rank was shown in a number of ways:

- **How they entered a room**. The aristocracy always entered first, followed by the landed gentry and their families. Families entered according to their age and marital status. Married women took precedence over single women, meaning that a younger sister could enter a room before her older sister once she was married (as Lydia is keen to do, entering before Jane in *Pride and Prejudice*).

- **How they were addressed**. People rarely used first names to address an acquaintance: only close friends and family did this. It was permissible for people of a higher rank to use the first name of a lower class friend (as shown with Emma and Harriet above), but not the other way around. The eldest daughter in a family was referred to as Miss (last name), while her sisters were called by their first names, so we meet Miss Elliot and Miss Anne. The same principle applied to sons, although most were referred to by their full name, so we are presented with Mr Ferrars (Edward) and Mr Robert Ferrars.

- **In meeting new people**. It was unacceptable just to walk up to someone and introduce yourself, unless you were from a higher rank. People of a lower or equal rank had to wait to be introduced by a friend or the master of ceremonies, or they were forced to remain silent, as Catherine and Mrs Allen are forced to do when they first arrive in Bath. After an introduction a person was always acknowledged as an acquaintance. If a person shunned an acquaintance it was called 'cutting' and was considered very rude.

Pocket Fact 🔱

After an introduction people would always acknowledge their acquaintance with another person, but only with a wave. Although nowadays people use a handshake to greet a new acquaintance, in the Regency period a handshake was only used among firm friends – hence Harriet's sense of honor when Emma shakes hands with her.

MANNERS FOR MEN

Young boys were taught to be 'gentlemen' from a very young age, both at home and at school. There were also guides available, called courtesy books, to teach young men how to behave. One popular guide was *Il Cortegiano*, an Italian courtesy guide for courtiers published in 1528, and translated into Latin and English by Sir Thomas Holby in 1561.

So exactly what manners and traits did a man have to possess to be considered a well-mannered gentleman? The essential parts of a gentleman's behavior dictated that he should:

- Speak and act confidently
- Use proper language and not make rude or vulgar remarks
- Be well-educated and able to give his opinion on all subjects
- Be well-turned out in his appearance
- Have a graceful walk and posture
- Be able to dance at balls
- Be polite and amiable with those of a lower class as well as those of his own class

So which of Austen's heroes fit this bill?

The perfect example of a gentleman in Austen's novels is Mr Knightley in Emma. *Mr Knightley always acts correctly, as we see when he behaves with condescension towards the poor*

> *Mrs and Miss Bates, when he walks and dances so well at the Crown Inn ball and because he also acts as a standard of moral good for Emma. Conversely Mr Darcy doesn't behave like a gentleman at all in* Pride *and* Prejudice. *He is rude to those whom he believes to be beneath him, and Elizabeth even chastises him for his complete lack of gentlemanly behavior. Unfortunately for poor Mr Knightley though, Mr Darcy was still the person a poll of almost 2,000 women voted as their ideal date.*

MANNERS FOR WOMEN

Women were expected to be meek, obedient, docile and soft. They were expected to take care with their appearance, and to obey the will of their fathers and then their husbands. Most gentry families would own copies of conduct manuals, such as Fordyce's *Sermons to Young Women* and Gregory's *A Father's Legacy to His Daughter*. These books advised young women to behave meekly and obediently, to value beauty over education and to hide any learning that they did have.

Austen mocks the accepted model of female behavior by having her heroines break with convention – and it would seem that they all manage to find the man of their dreams by behaving in a manner which departs from the norm:

- **Elizabeth Bennet: too forthright**. By speaking her mind and not living up to the simpering female model he is used to, Darcy finds Elizabeth captivating for her differences.

- **Catherine Morland: too open**. Catherine never conceals her regard for Henry and it is her blatant preference for him that makes Henry notice her in the first place.

- **Emma Woodhouse: in charge of her life and household.** Emma's independent wealth means she doesn't need a husband and never seeks one until she realizes she is in love with Mr Knightley.

- **Anne Elliot: being constant to her first love.** Although Anne is forced to break off her engagement with Captain

Wentworth she declines an offer from Charles Musgrove, a wealthy man who would help Anne fulfill her duty of marrying well, because her feelings remain true to Captain Wentworth.

- **Marianne Dashwood: too emotional and free-spirited.** Although Marianne's lack of secrecy about her feelings proves to be disastrous in her relationship with Willoughby, her openness and free-spirited behavior remind Colonel Brandon of his first love and endears Marianne to him from the start.

- **Fanny Price: doesn't hunt for a husband.** Fanny secretly pines for Edmund throughout the entirety of *Mansfield Park*, and even when she is sure he is going to marry Mary Crawford, she won't accept Henry Crawford's offer of marriage even though it would give her security for life.

❧ FEATURES OF REGENCY ❧ SOCIETY

WEALTH, LAND AND INHERITANCE

Traditionally, gentlemen made their career and their fortune from their estate. Estates were inherited and provided a family's wealth and social status. The eldest son of a gentry family would normally make his career the management of the estate, overseeing the tenants and the farming. Many eldest sons had to wait a long time to take on this role though, leaving them free to lead a lazy existence, sure of their future inheritance. Take Tom Bertram in *Mansfield Park* and Willoughby in *Sense and Sensibility* for example. However, some young men found this lifestyle curtailed by the need to pander to the relative who controlled their inheritance, as we see with Frank Churchill and his demanding aunt in *Emma*.

In Her Own Words 🖫

Jane was critical of the laziness arising from this line of 'career', as can be seen in Elinor's reflection on Willoughby's behavior in Sense and Sensibility: *'Her thoughts were silently fixed on the irreparable injury which too early an independence and its consequent habits of idleness, dissipation, and luxury, had made in the mind, the character, the happiness, of a man who, to every advantage of person and talents, united a disposition naturally open and honest and a feeling, affectionate temper. The world had made him extravagant and vain — extravagance and vanity had made him cold-hearted and selfish.'*

The size of the estate had a lot to do with the wealth of the family. Mr Darcy's estate Pemberley is worth £10,000 a year (about $512,000 now), whereas Mr Bennet's estate of Longbourn is worth only £2,000 (about $102,000 now). A father would have to support his family using this income, as well as provide a dowry for his daughter. This is why the daughters of large estates were targeted by ambitious young men, as the control of their wealth and any property they would inherit would pass to them after their marriage. (See p. 44 for the wealthiest estates in Jane's novels.)

CAREERS

If the eldest sons in gentry families inherited the family estate and made their career managing these estates, what did younger sons do? There were several respectable careers a younger son could pursue and still retain the respectable appearance of a gentleman. The main choices for a younger son were either to become a lawyer, enter the church or join the army. Of course some elder sons also chose to pursue careers in these professions, while they waited to inherit their property.

'A person who can write a long letter with ease, cannot write ill': *Communicating by letter*

During Jane's lifetime the only mode of communication available was the letter. This meant that the only news people had of their loved ones came infrequently and due to the unreliability of the mail could often be out of date by the time it arrived.

When writing a letter people would use a quill pen and the writing paper would be folded, leaving one blank page for the address. People would try to fit as much writing as possible on a page, to save on both the cost of paper and the price of postage (although at that time the recipient of the letter would pay the postage). People often employed a method called 'cross writing' to save space; once a page was filled people would turn the page on its side at a right angle and write between the lines of text already written. When the letter was finished it would be sealed with a wax seal.

Letters play an important part in Jane's novels, often revealing key information or acting as the vehicle for an expression of love. See if you can spot the important role letters play in Austen's novels.

THE DAY IN THE LIFE OF A YOUNG LADY

Young ladies were expected to be 'accomplished'. While Jane makes fun of this concept in *Pride and Prejudice* it was a fact of life that young ladies, to be good marriage material, had to posses certain skills. A young lady in Jane's time would fill her day with the following activities: writing letters, learning French, drawing, sewing, reading novels or conduct guides, planning meals (if their mothers weren't alive), making tea for visitors or paying morning visits to friends, and practising a musical instrument: usually the harp or the pianoforte. Austen herself was a talented pianist who practised every day before she began her writing.

It was these types of accomplishments that most young ladies would learn to do, in place of a formal education. Young women would receive some education from a governess or at a boarding school but most of their education focused on running a household.

Regency Fashion

We've all seen the bonnets worn in the films, and heard Caroline Bingley's shock at the state of Elizabeth's petticoat, but do you know exactly what was considered fashionable for a Regency lady? Here's a list of everything you would need to be considered well dressed:

- **Dress**. A lady's dress would be straight with short sleeves, a high waistline and a low neckline. Dresses often had a train but this fashion was beginning to die out during Austen's time. Dresses were made from a fine cotton material called muslin and were usually white or a light pastel color with a floral design. Having a white dress was a sign of status and wealth.
- **Undergarments**. A lady would need at least one petticoat with a pair of long drawers and a chemise (like a slip).
- **Hairstyle.** A lady's hair was worn up with short curls at the front.
- **Evening dress.** For the evening ladies would wear a similar style dress, more often with a train and more ornate decoration. They would wear simple jewelry, carry a fan and wear gloves. They might also decorate their hair with feathers or ribbons.
- **Outerwear**. Ladies would often wear a shawl around their shoulders, and would wear a bonnet when venturing outside. In colder weather they could wear a spencer (a tight fitting waist-length jacket, like a man's coat but without tails) or a pelisse (a long dress-like coat often lined with fur). They would wear gloves and might also carry a muff.

Pocket Fact 🕯️

From all accounts it seems that Jane didn't really care about her dress or her appearance. She once wrote to Cassandra saying, 'My hair was at least tidy which was all my ambition' and in Northanger Abbey the narrator points out that, 'It would be mortifying to the feelings of many ladies, could they be made to understand how little the heart of man is affected by what is costly or new in their attire . . . woman is fine for her own satisfaction alone.'

A woman needed to have enough of a dowry to be considered a good match. If a woman from a lower gentry family couldn't find a man willing to accept her lack of fortune and marry her she was left with the prospect of becoming a spinster. Jane and her sister Cassandra both chose this path, meaning they had to live on their brothers' generosity rather than being provided for by a husband. If a woman didn't have a kind brother or family member to support her most often she would have been forced into a career as a governess.

Governesses were pitiful figures, as they were above the other servants in the house but couldn't mix socially with the family and their guests. Women were aware that being a governess was a lonely life, and Jane Fairfax, who is facing the prospect of becoming a governess, compares it to a state of slavery, saying 'There are places in town, offices . . . offices for the sale, not quite of human flesh, but of human intellect' (see p. 79 for more on this).

SOCIAL EVENTS

Dances

Dances were a major part of Regency society. Dances and balls were held both at public assembly rooms, and at private residences. It was also not uncommon at family parties for the young people to roll back the carpet and dance to whatever instrument they had in the home.

Pocket Fact 👖

Henry Austen recalled that 'Jane was fond of dancing and excelled in it'.

Dances were the best, and very nearly the only, way for young people to meet and get to know each other. In essence a dance was the best place to find a spouse. Dancing together was the only acceptable way for young people to have a private conversation. It was normal for dancing lessons to be a part of a genteel boy or girl's education and being able to dance was considered a necessary social skill.

In Her Own Words 🔱

Jane clearly acknowledged the importance of dancing in finding a partner, as seen by Henry Tilney's analogy in Northanger Abbey: *'I consider a country-dance as an emblem of marriage. Fidelity and complaisance are the principal duties of both.'*

So what exactly happened at a dance?

- A gentleman would ask a lady to dance (but only if he had been properly introduced by a mutual acquaintance or the master of ceremonies).

- The most important lady in the room (the one of the highest social rank) would open the first set.

- The dance would most likely be a country dance, such as a minuet, a quadrille, a cotillion, or a Scottish reel (see the glossary for more on these dances).

- The dance would consist of sets of five to eight couples.

- The couples would stand opposite each other in two lines.

- Each dance would last about half an hour.

- A couple couldn't dance together more than twice, or it was thought that there was a decided engagement between them.

- The ball itself would last from 8 pm until 3 or 4 am!

Pocket Fact 🔱

Although dances and balls feature prominently in all of Jane's novels she never specifically names the dances her couples are performing.

Evenings

If they weren't at a dance a Regency family would spend their evening in one of the following ways:

- Playing cards
- Reading aloud to one another
- Listening to one of the daughters play an instrument
- Putting on a play
- Making conversation on the issues of the day

Dinners

A Regency dinner party would have begun between 5 and 6 pm (although the acceptable time for dinner would differ between the country and London), starting with soup, followed by a main course of meat, surrounded by jellies, quinces, vegetables, and a number of other dishes. After the main course, salad and cheese would be served. There would then be a second main course with several different types of dishes. After this the tablecloth was removed (hence Austen's use of the phrase 'the cloth was removed') and dessert was served.

After the meal the ladies would go to the drawing room to sew and chat, while the gentlemen stayed in the dining room to drink port, and possibly smoke cigars. The gentlemen would then join the ladies for cards and tea.

People would always dress formally for dinner, even if they had been dressed nicely all day. This meant that ladies wore more elaborate dresses and men would wear white shirts and waistcoats and change their riding boots and jacket for formal ones.

Planning your own Regency dinner party

Food

To start serve soup, such as a white soup made from veal or chicken stock, egg yolks, ground almonds and cream, or even a mock turtle soup.

For a main course offer something like roast chicken with egg sauce, or mutton. For dessert try baked apples, rum cake or rice pudding.

Entertainment

Card games were a popular pastime after dinner. Here are a few you can try:

- Cassino (fishing card game for two partnerships of two, three or four players)

- Loo (a gambling game for five or more players)

- Piquet (a card dealing game for only two players)

- Quadrille (a trick taking card game, developed from Whist, for four players)

- Speculation (a gambling game which involves a whole deck of cards for any number of players)

You can also try playing the pianoforte, or having an impromptu dance. Charades were also a popular game, using written rhymes which gave clues to the answer as we see Emma and Harriet compiling in *Emma*.

Some Austen stereotypes to invite
To have a true Austen style dinner party there are a few stereotypical characters you'll need to invite:

- **A spinster (like Miss Bates)**
  Pro: She will keep the conversation going.
  Con: You might be left with an odd number.

- **An elderly relative (like Mr Woodhouse)**
  Pro: He or she will praise your planning and musical performance after the meal.
  Con: He or she will want the party to finish early.

- **An annoying neighbor and his wife (like Mr and Mrs Elton)**
  Pro: You will fulfill your obligation to invite them and seem a gracious host.
  Con: You will have to put up with their boastful conversation.

- **The local clergyman (like Mr Collins)**
  Pro: He could be a potential catch for your friend.
  Con: He may be boring or have designs on you which you will have to politely decline.

- **Your best friend (like Charlotte Lucas)**
  Pro: You will have someone there to talk about your guests with.
  Con: She may distract the eligible bachelor.

- **The local militia (like Wickham)**
  Pro: Attractive young men who will join in the dancing and flirt with your female guests.
  Con: They may be scoundrels in disguise.

- **The eligible bachelor (like Charles Bingley)**
  Pro: This is the man you have your eye on so it's a chance to get to know him better.
  Con: You will have to make sure you are sitting near him and be charming all night long.

- **Your family and near neighbors (like the Bennets and the Lucases)**
  Pro: They make up numbers.
  Con: You might be embarrassed by them.

Pocket Fact 🕯

During World War One British soldiers suffering from shell shock were advised to read Austen's novels. The hope was that the comforting images of idyllic English society would help speed up their recovery.

🐚 JANE AUSTEN TODAY 🐚

Nowadays Jane Austen is hugely popular with both casual readers and academics, and her work and life inspires societies and clubs for people from all walks of life. Jane Austen features on English literature courses all over the world and her novels have never been out of print since they were first published nearly 200 years ago.

Here are just a few examples of Jane's enduring popularity:

- In 2002 Jane was voted number 70 in the BBC's top 100 Britons.

- In 2003 Jane had three novels appear in the BBC's Big Read poll, a list of the greatest books of all time. *Emma* came in at 40, *Persuasion* appeared at 38, and *Pride and Prejudice* was voted number 2.

- A poll conducted by Woman's Hour on BBC Radio 4 identified that 93% of women said that *Pride and Prejudice* was the book they could relate to most.

Pocket Fact ♆

Not everyone is a fan of Jane Austen. The author Mark Twain openly hated Jane Austen, and was quoted as saying, 'Every time I read Pride and Prejudice *I want to dig her up and hit her over the head with her shin bone.'*

3

'There is nothing like staying at home for real comfort': Austen's geography

The geography of Austen's life can provide a great insight into the settings and events of her novels. For example, Austen's dislike of Bath is shared by Anne Elliot in *Persuasion*, and Highbury village where Emma lives shares similarities with Steventon where Austen spent her childhood. The grand country estates and locations used in the film and television adaptations of Austen's novels also provide feelings of romantic aspiration, as we can try to picture ourselves wandering the grounds of Pemberley while visiting Chatsworth house, the place which is thought to have inspired Austen.

✿ PLACES AUSTEN LIVED ✿

STEVENTON RECTORY, HAMPSHIRE

Jane was born at the Steventon rectory where she lived until she was 25 (1775–1801). The rectory was a 17th century house with large fields and a farm attached to it. It was a short walk to the village of Steventon and the Church of St Nicholas where Jane's father was rector. While Steventon rectory is no longer there, you can visit the site where it stood, as well as St Nicholas' Church (which burned down and was rebuilt in 1872) where Jane was christened on April 5 1776.

In Her Own Words 🌑

Jane didn't spend all her time at Steventon when she was young. She also went to visit her brother Henry in London, but as her letters show she wasn't too thrilled with her destination: 'Here I am once more in this scene of dissipation and vice, and I begin already to find my morals corrupted.' (Letter on arriving in London, 1796)

BATH

In 1800 Jane's father decided to retire, deciding that he, his wife and his two daughters should move to Bath. Jane's parents had met and married in Bath so it makes sense that they wanted to return there for their retirement. Moving from their comfortable family home in the country to smaller rented premises in the city meant that the Austens had to sell their pianoforte as well as Mr Austen's entire library, and live in the bustle of a busy city instead of enjoying the open countryside.

In Her Own Words 🌑

Austen described Bath as 'vapor, shadow, smoke & confusion'.

Jane, her parents and her sister Cassandra arrived at rented accommodation in Bath in May 1801. By September they had managed to find a permanent place to live, and soon moved to 4 Sydney Place. This house still stands in Bath, with a plaque commemorating Jane's life there. While living in Bath Jane enjoyed a busy social life, full of dances, visits to the theater and the Pump Rooms (the rooms built above the Roman baths – from which Bath gets its name – where well-to-do residents would go to socialize and partake of the mineral waters – see the glossary), and walking around the city. Her family also traveled extensively during this period, visiting their extended family and enjoying trips to the coast.

SOUTHAMPTON AND GODMERSHAM

In 1805 Jane's father died. Jane and her mother and sister now found themselves in a poor financial situation, having to get by with very little income. Jane's brothers all started to chip in to support their mother and sisters. The women stayed at the rented house in Bath until 1806 when they began to move between the Austen brothers and their families. In 1806 the women moved to Southampton to live with Frank Austen and his new wife and in 1808 Jane went to Godmersham, her brother Edward's estate in Kent.

Pocket Fact 🕎

There are no surviving manuscripts of either the drafts or the final novels for any of Austen's published novels: the only draft writing we have is the original ending of Persuasion. *Considering that Jane's early novels traveled between Steventon, Bath, Godmersham and Hampshire, it is impressive that they were not lost altogether.*

CHAWTON

In 1808, following the death of his wife during childbirth, Edward invited his mother and sisters to live at a cottage in the grounds of his other estate Chawton in Hampshire. The six bedroom red brick cottage was close to Steventon, where Jane's brother James was now the rector, and the women happily moved into the cottage. The cottage was close to the main road and the noise of the carriages passing on their way to and from London was a common feature.

This cottage at Chawton proved to be the most conducive location for Jane's work, as she published four novels, completed one, and began another while living here.

Pocket Fact 🕎

After the publication of Pride and Prejudice *in 1813, Jane's mother began reading the novel aloud to Miss Benn, a guest who was staying at Chawton. Miss Benn was completely unaware that she was in the author's presence while she was listening to the story, but Jane's only complaint was that her mother read too quickly and didn't get the characters' voices right.*

WINCHESTER

In 1816 Jane began to feel increasingly unwell and was so weak she had to stop writing. In May 1817 Jane was taken to Winchester in south-east England to be near her doctor, Giles King Lyford. She and her family moved to 10 College Street to live with their old friends the Biggs, but Jane's health decreased rapidly. She died peacefully in July 1817. Using their clerical connections her brother Henry arranged for her to be buried in Winchester Cathedral.

Austen tour of England

For the true Austen fan, a tour of the places Austen lived or used as the settings for her novels can provide a real insight into their favorite author. Try this whistle-stop tour of Austen's England:

- *Go to Steventon in Hampshire to see the village where Jane was born and spent her childhood. Wander around the streets of Steventon and try to imagine Highbury forming in Jane's mind.*
- *Visit Bath to see the Pump Rooms and Assembly Rooms featured in* Northanger Abbey, *and where Austen herself attended social events.*
- *Visit Chawton to see where Austen spent the last days of her life.*
- *Go to Winchester Cathedral to see Austen's grave, which doesn't mention the fact that she was a writer.*
- *Go to Lyme Regis and demand to see where Lousia Musgrove fell, just like Lord Tennyson did on his visit.*
- *Go to Derbyshire and see Chatsworth, which is thought to have inspired Pemberley.*
- *Go to the British Museum in London and see Jane's writing desk.*
- *Visit 10 Henrietta Street in Covent Garden in London where Jane visited her brother Henry.*

> • *Follow Lydia and Wickham's route when they eloped – from Brighton through Epsom, to Clapham in London, and then to the church of St Clement's, only to be discovered by Darcy and forced to move to Newcastle.*

🐚 SETTINGS FOR NOVELS 🐚

The various locations and country estates found in Austen's novels can be as intriguing to readers as the romantic plots. This section gives an oversight of the locations found in Austen's novels, allowing you to plan your own tour of the real places featured in Austen's novels, or to imagine yourself wandering the halls of the great country houses she creates for her characters.

SENSE AND SENSIBILITY

Norland Park, Sussex: The Dashwood home.

Barton Park and Barton Cottage, Devonshire: The home of Sir John Middleton and the Dashwood women respectively.

Delaford, Devonshire: The home of Colonel Brandon, and eventually Marianne.

Combe Magna, Somersetshire: Willoughby's estate.

Berkeley Street, London: Mrs Jennings' home in London.

Allenham, Devonshire: The estate Willoughby is set to inherit.

Cleveland, Somersetshire: The Palmer's estate where Marianne falls ill.

PRIDE AND PREJUDICE

Longbourn, Hertfordshire: The Bennets' home.

Netherfield, Hertfordshire: Mr Bingley's rented estate.

Lucas Lodge, Hertfordshire: The home of Sir William Lucas and his family.

Meryton, Hertfordshire: The village near Longbourn, where the Bennet girls often walk.

Pemberley, Derbyshire: Darcy's vast estate.

Rosings Park, Kent: Lady Catherine de Bourgh's estate.

Hunsford, Kent: The parsonage Mr Collins holds at Rosings.

Gracechurch Street, London: The home of Mr and Mrs Gardiner.

Brighton, Sussex: Where Lydia goes and then runs away from with Wickham.

MANSFIELD PARK

Mansfield Park: The home of the Bertram family and Fanny Price.

Mansfield Parsonage: The parsonage where Mr and Mrs Norris, and then the Grants live. This is also where Mary and Henry Crawford live on their visit.

Sotherton: Mr Rushworth's estate.

Portsmouth: Where Fanny's family lives and where she returns on a visit.

Antigua: Sir Thomas has a plantation here and he goes to oversee the business for a time.

London: Where both Maria and Julia elope from.

Thornton Lacey: The clerical living Edmund is set to receive.

EMMA

Hartfield, Surrey: The home of Mr Woodhouse and Emma. Mr Knightley also lives there when he marries Emma.

Randalls, Surrey: The home of Mr and Mrs Weston.

Highbury, Surrey: The village near to Hartfield, Randalls and Donwell Abbey.

Donwell Abbey, Surrey: Mr Knightley's estate.

Brunswick Square, London: The home of John Knightley and his wife Isabella.

Bath: Where Mr Elton goes to meet his wife.

Richmond, London: Where Mrs Churchill goes for her health.

Southend, Essex: Where Isabella and John take their children for sea bathing.

Weymouth, Dorset: Where Jane Fairfax and Frank Churchill first meet.

NORTHANGER ABBEY

Fullerton, Wiltshire: The village where Catherine Morland is from.

Bath: The city Catherine goes to visit and where she meets Henry Tilney.

Northanger Abbey, Gloucestershire: The home of the Tilney family.

Oxford: Where Catherine's brother James goes to university.

Putney, London: Where the Thorpe family are from.

PERSUASION

Kellynch Hall: The home of the Elliot family, which they are forced to let out to Admiral Croft.

Uppercross: The home of the Musgrove family.

Lyme Regis: The seaside town where Louisa Musgrove is injured and then falls in love with Captain Benwick.

Bath: The city the Elliots move to, and where Anne is finally united with Captain Wentworth.

Real places that inspired Austen

Although most of the grand estates found in Austen's novels are fictional places, there are a few real locations which inspired her:

- **Chatsworth House for Pemberley**. *Austen's description of Pemberley in* Pride and Prejudice *is widely thought to have been inspired by Chatsworth house.*

- **Lyme Regis**. *In 1803 and 1804 Austen visited Lyme Regis in West Dorset on three separate occasions with her family. She was inspired by the seaside town, 'The Cobb' and the harbor wall, and the town itself features prominently in* Persuasion.
- **Bath**. *Jane lived in Bath for several years and the scenes from* Northanger Abbey *and* Persuasion *featuring the Assembly Rooms, the Pump Rooms or the Royal Crescent would have been experienced by Jane herself in that exact location.*
- **Cottesbrooke Hall for Mansfield Park**. *Jane would have received descriptions of this country house in Northamptonshire from her brother Henry, who was acquainted with the Langham family who owned the property.*

✿ 'THE SHADES OF PEMBERLEY': ✿ 10 LUXURIOUS HOUSES AND ESTATES IN AUSTEN'S NOVELS

Pemberley

Location: Derbyshire

Income: £10,000 a year (about $512,000 now)

Real place: Chatsworth house

Fact: It is on visiting Pemberley, seeing the grounds and listening to the housekeeper's account of Darcy, that Elizabeth begins to change her mind about him.

Rosings Park

Location: Kent

Income: Considerable – we are told (by Mr Collins) that the chimney piece alone cost £800 (about $41,000 now).

Real place: Chevening is thought to have inspired Rosings.

Donwell Abbey

Location: Surrey

Size: We're told that most of Hartfield village and the surrounding farmland is part of the estate.

Fact: It is meant to be famous for its strawberry beds and apples.

Northanger Abbey

Location: Somerset, 30 miles from Bath

Income: Enough to provide a respectable inheritance for Frederick Tinley, a large dowry for Eleanor and to buy and furnish a parsonage for Henry.

Fact: Although the Abbey becomes the focus of Catherine's wild Gothic fancies, the building itself is described as thoroughly modern.

Kellynch Hall

Location: Somerset, 50 miles from Bath.

Size: We are told that Mary scoffs at Winthrop which is 250 acres, so Kellynch must be considerably larger.

Fact: Kellynch Hall is full of mirrors, which the Admiral confesses he has covered up!

Delaford House

Location: Dorsetshire

Income: £2,000 a year (about $102,000 now)

Size: We are told the house contains five sitting rooms and space for 15 beds.

Fact: Part of the estate is the Delaford rectory, which Colonel Brandon gives to Edward when he is cut off from his family. Edward and Elinor both settle there after their marriage.

Hartfield

Location: Surrey

Income: We are not told Mr Woodhouse's income but it is large enough that Emma does not need to marry.

Size: The house itself is described as large and modern, but there is only a small garden.

Fact: Mr Knightley gives up his home at Donwell to move to Hartfield so that he and Emma can marry without leaving the invalid Mr Woodhouse alone in Hartfield.

Longbourn House

Location: Hertfordshire

Income: £2,000 a year (about $102,000 now)

Size: The house has eight rooms (that we are told of), including a library. There is also a garden with a walk leading to a 'wilderness' garden.

Fact: Mr Collins will inherit Longbourn as the estate is entailed to male descendants only.

Netherfield Park

Location: Hertfordshire

Income: Enough to tempt Mr Bingley with an income of £4,000 a year (about $205,000 now).

Size: Bingley is able to throw a ball for the whole local society.

Fact: Jane and Bingley live in Netherfield when they are newly married, but find it is too close to Jane's family at Longbourn so they move to Derbyshire.

Barton Park

Location: In Barton Valley, Devonshire

Income: We are told Sir John is a man of consequence and large property, and he is able to host guests and parties all year round.

Size: Large enough to accommodate lots of guests and to host balls on a regular basis.

Fact: We are told that the valley in which the Park and Barton cottage is situated is very beautiful, and it is the setting for Marianne's romantic meeting with Willoughby.

Austen museums to visit

The Jane Austen House Museum, Chawton

Located in Chawton, the Jane Austen House Museum is housed in the cottage Jane lived in between 1808 and 1817. The museum contains letters written by Jane, a quilt she embroidered for her mother and the table she sat at to write. You can walk in the gardens and there is a shop where you can buy all things Austen.

Nearby, Chawton House is now home to the The Centre for the Study of Early English Women's Writing, 1600–1830, which runs programs associated with the University of Southampton. The two houses are run by separate charities but do work together to promote Jane and her works. While visiting Chawton it is also possible to walk to the St Nicholas Church where Jane's mother and sister are buried.

The Jane Austen Centre, Bath

This museum in Bath is located at 40 Gay Street, a few doors down from where Austen herself lived at number 25 between 1800 and 1808. The center has a permanent exhibition which features costumes, letters, films and maps. There is also a Regency tea room and a gift shop. The center runs walking tours of Bath highlighting the places Jane lived, and the settings for Persuasion and Northanger Abbey.

4

'A woman, especially if she have the misfortune of knowing anything, should conceal it as well as she can':
Influences and literary context

Why did Jane Austen never publish her novels under her own name? And why did she feel the need to launch a defense of her chosen form in *Northanger Abbey*, a story which in itself mocks the popular Gothic form? This chapter takes you through the literary context Jane Austen was writing in, looking at the writers who influenced her, the styles of writing which were prevalent at the time, and the place of women writers.

🐚 THE RISE OF THE NOVEL 🐚

The novel was a relatively new style of writing which was growing in popularity, though not in reputation, during Jane's lifetime. The novel had grown from the medieval romances of the 12th century (such as Thomas Malory's *Le Morte d'Arthur*) and consisted of a few key elements:

- Novels were prose works, longer in length than poetry or drama.

- They contained realistic characters who led real lives.

- They were intended to teach the reader a moral lesson through the experiences of the characters.

The novel genre saw a surge in popularity as a result of a combination of events:

- Cheaper printing technology meant longer works could be printed in higher volumes.

- There was a rise in literacy levels throughout society.

- The move away from manual labor meant people, especially women, of the middle and upper classes had more free time.

- The rise of the circulating library (a service like a public library where readers could order and access books, see p. 51 for more) meant that people who couldn't afford to buy books were still able to read and enjoy novels.

Although the novel grew rapidly in popularity, the form wasn't respected by intellectuals and the upper classes, and was deemed the cheap entertainment of the masses. Samuel Taylor Coleridge, one of the leading poets of the day, claimed that, 'where the reading of novels prevails as a habit, it occasions in time the entire destruction of the powers of the mind'. It was put forth that the novel could never rival the high-brow content of more established forms such as poetry, history or drama, and the form certainly wasn't helped by the rise of the Gothic novel (see p. 52) or by the rise of women writers (see p. 54).

In Her Own Words ●

'Our family are great Novel-readers and not ashamed of being so.' (Letter to Cassandra, 1798)

However, Austen (as a female author and a fan of novels) defends her chosen form of writing and makes sure to parody those more respected forms of writing, or those novel forms that diminish the reputation of the genre.

Here are just a few examples of the forms Austen mocks:

- **Histories**. Jane's early work *The History of England* was a parody of Oliver Goldsmith's work of the same name.

- **Novels of sensibility**. The overly sensitive and emotional character of Marianne Dashwood is Jane's satire of the sentimental and moralistic works which grew out of the Age of Sensibility.

- **Conduct guides**. Austen mocks the conduct guides that attempted to educate young women on proper behavior, such as Fordyce and Gregory, by presenting female heroines who consistently break with convention, and are usually rewarded for doing so by winning the attentions of their future husbands (see p. 26).

In Her Own Words

In discussing novels Jane said, 'If a book is well written, I always find it too short'.

❦ WHO INSPIRED JANE AUSTEN? ❦

While a lot of Austen's work parodies and mocks the popular forms of her day, she is also careful to praise and emulate the forms she respects and likes. Here are Jane's favorite authors and forms, and the influence they had on her work:

- **Shakespeare**. Jane was a fan of Shakespeare and her family would often read his plays aloud in the evenings. We can see the influence of Shakespeare on Jane's work in her dramatic representation of events, and the amount of dialogue she uses. Jane also mentions Shakespeare explicitly in *Mansfield Park* when Fanny is impressed by Henry's reading of *Henry VIII*.

- **Dr Johnson**. Jane fought against the sentimental notions of the Age of Sensibility and instead followed the model espoused by Samuel Johnson, emphasizing the importance of self knowledge and reason. Austen's sensible and reasonable characters, such as Elinor Dashwood and Anne Elliot, are aware of their own character and so can behave properly and admirably in any situation.

- **Samuel Richardson**. Richardson's novel *The History of Sir Charles Grandison* was one of Jane's favorites as a child, and this, along with some of his other works, prompted Jane to emulate his style, first by writing *First Impressions* and *Elinor and Marianne* in epistolary form, and even attempting a play called *Sir Charles Grandison or the happy man*. Although Jane also follows the model of Richardson's 1740 novel *Pamela* in all of her own novels, she doesn't use the extreme situations Richardson portrays to evoke sympathy, instead presenting her heroines in everyday situations, and gaining sympathy from her readers from the relatable nature of their experiences.

- **Laurence Sterne**. Another author of sentimental prose whom Austen admired.

- **William Cowper**. Jane was a big fan of Cowper's poetry, such as *The Task*, and she mentions his poetry in *Persuasion* and *Sense and Sensibility*.

🐚 THE CIRCULATING LIBRARY 🐚 AND FEMALE READERS

The rise of the novel was helped significantly by the rise in both female readers and the related rise of the circulating library, which allowed these women access to novels. The circulating library (a service a bit like a public library where readers paid a fee to access books) became widely popular in the 18th century, with almost 1,000 established in England by 1801. These libraries allowed readers to subscribe for a fee and borrow a specific number of books at a time, depending on the fee paid. This access to books meant that novels became popular at a time when most people couldn't afford to buy books. Novels were an easy pleasure, a book read once and forgotten. Therefore people were more willing to rent novels than buy them, as Austen herself observed, 'People are more ready to borrow and praise, than to buy – which I cannot wonder at'. Most first editions of novels published found themselves in circulating libraries, and most of the stock of these libraries was made up of fiction.

For women, who had very little disposable income of their own, circulating libraries offered access to the growing number of novels that were being manufactured for this contingent audience of women readers. Austen's description in Mansfield Park of Fanny joining the circulating library shows how the circulating library became a new found means of intellectual freedom for women: 'She became a subscriber . . . to be a renter, a chuser of books! And to be having any one's improvement in view of her choice!' As circulating libraries made novels widely available they became subject to the same prejudice and scorn faced by the novels themselves. The fact that women were getting increased access to the forms which were deemed unworthy for reading, meant that the reputation of the novel, and the type of women who read them, fell lower still.

Pocket Fact 👑

In an experiment carried out by the director of the Jane Austen festival, several chapters of Pride and Prejudice, Northanger Abbey *and* Persuasion *were submitted to various publishers under the name 'Alison Laydee' (a play on Austen's pseudonym 'A Lady') with only minor alterations and the original titles Austen had given them. All of the submissions were rejected. It seems that Jane Austen may have struggled to find a publisher in today's market as well!*

🐚 THE GOTHIC NOVEL 🐚

The rise of the Gothic novel in the 18th century began with Horace Walpole's novel *The Castle of Otranto* (1765), which combined Gothic settings with thrilling horror and supernatural events. The arising genre combined themes of horror and romance in a way calculated to evoke a sense of pleasing terror. Walpole's work contained elements of melodrama, and a prevalence of emotion and atmosphere which reflected a rejection of the Enlightenment ideals. This new genre came about during a revival in Gothic architecture, which saw the literature evoke the very crumbling, ancient buildings they were set in. Gothic fiction often contained elements of the supernatural, terrible family secrets, and female victims locked up by evil tyrants in castles.

In the 1740s Samuel Richardson's and Henry Fielding's novels and their 'literary realism' had made the genre acceptable, but the supernatural elements of Gothic fiction relegated the form back into populist trash. In the 1790s Ann Radcliffe managed to rescue the reputation of the Gothic novel, by explaining the supernatural. Her novels, full of natural causes for seemingly supernatural events, experienced by morally superior heroines, began to make the Gothic form acceptable. However Radcliffe's success had an unforeseen consequence in that the market became flooded with cheap, low quality imitations, meaning the inferior reputation of Gothic fiction remained.

Pocket Fact 💥

Richard Sheridan, author of The Rivals, *which Jane had performed at Steventon as a child, described* Pride *and* Prejudice *as 'one of the cleverest things' he had ever read.*

The outlandish stereotypical elements of Gothic fiction meant that its characters and plots were perfect for parody and satire. This was exactly Austen's intent in writing *Northanger Abbey*. Her heroine Catherine Morland portrays the danger of being carried away by the emotional melodrama of Gothic fiction, as her imagination runs away with her while she is staying at the Abbey. In her novel Austen mentions some of the most famous Gothic novels of the day, including:

- *The Monk* by M G Lewis
- *The Mysteries of Udolpho* by Ann Radcliffe
- *The Italian*, also by Ann Radcliffe

Her mocking of the Gothic form shows that while Austen is a champion for the novel form, she does not want to be associated with the low reputation of the Gothic. Jane does use her parody to launch a defense of the novel form, as seen in her authorial aside, when describing Catherine and Isabella's reading:

'Yes, novels; – for I will not adopt that ungenerous and impolitic custom so common with novel-writers, of degrading by their contemptuous censure the very performances, to the number of which they are themselves adding – joining with their greatest enemies in bestowing the harshest epithets on such works, and scarcely ever permitting them to be read by their own heroine, who, if she accidentally take up a novel, is sure to turn over its insipid pages with disgust. Alas! if the heroine of one novel be not patronized by the heroine of another, from whom can she expect protection and regard? I cannot approve of it.'

FEMALE WRITERS

While the novel genre, aimed mainly at female readers, was on the rise, this period also saw a rise in the opportunities for women writers. The female novelists who became popular at this time created both a market and an audience for Jane Austen. Many of these contemporary novelists were better known than Austen (who published anonymously) but this meant that they faced the sullied reputation of being a female author.

Society deemed it unladylike for women to pursue fame and a profitable career, meaning many female writers, including Austen herself, decided to publish their novels anonymously to avoid the slander that could accompany their name. Many women were discouraged from writing by their husbands and families. Jane was lucky in this respect as her father encouraged her writing and even approached a publisher for her when she was 22. Jane's brother also acted as her representative at her publisher when her novels did get published.

Although there was a stigma attached to being a female author, during this time it was relatively easy to be published. Writers had four main options to get their work into print:

- **Publishing by subscription**. This method meant that people would sign up to receive a proposed novel. Once enough subscriptions had been received a novel would be put into print and sent out to the subscribers.

- **Publishing by profit sharing**. This meant that the publisher paid for the publication of a novel but the author only received a fee once the book had made a profit. If a book didn't sell well enough to make a profit the author got nothing.

- **Publishing by selling the copyright.** Most new authors chose this method, selling their copyright for a small fee in return for having their work published. This was a gamble; if the novel did well they only received their initial fee but it removed the risk of a failure.

- **Publishing on commission**. This method meant that an author paid all the costs for the publication of a book, and the publisher acted as the distributor. The publisher would also take a 10% fee from the profits of the book. If the book made a loss the author would have to pay for this. This is the option which Jane herself chose.

So while being a female author could attract a poor reputation, the growing opportunities for publication, along with the growth of a female audience meant that female authors began to be a firm presence in the market. It was this market that Jane was determined to be a part of, trying all her life to get her work published. This was a goal she finally achieved at the age of 34.

FEMALE NOVELISTS WHO INSPIRED AUSTEN

- **Frances Burney**. Burney was the author of *Cecilia*, *Camilla* and *Evelina*. These novels all showed young women interacting with family and friends in real circumstances. Jane read these comedies of manners in her youth and their heavy influence on her novels is clear to see.

Pocket Fact 𝖜

Jane subscribed to Burney's novel Cecilia *when she was 20. The phrase 'Pride and Prejudice' appears in this novel several times so it's probable that this is where Jane found the title of her novel.*

- **Mary Wollstonecraft**. Wollstonecraft was an active advocate of women's rights at this time. She wrote *A Vindication of the Rights of Woman* in 1792 and also criticized Dr James Fordyce's conduct guides for demeaning women. She claimed that women were rational creatures ruined by the patriarchal system.

The character of Mrs Croft in *Persuasion* espouses exactly this sentiment.

- **Ann Radcliffe**. Mrs Radcliffe's novels were responsible for the validation of the Gothic novel and she gained fame as the author of popular works such as *The Castle of Udolpho*. She published under her own name, Mrs Radcliffe, but her marital status meant that her husband received all of her profits and copyright fees.

- **Maria Edgeworth**. Edgeworth wrote several novels as well as children's literature, and was respected by male contemporaries such as Walter Scott. Edgeworth was interested in the issue of education and put forward the argument that children should be allowed to be free to make mistakes and learn from them. We can see the influence of this thinking in Austen's work when we consider that all of Jane's heroines go through this kind of learning process.

⚜ AUSTEN'S RECEPTION ⚜

At the time of their publication Jane's novels were considered fashionable and drew admiration from Princess Charlotte, the daughter of the Prince Regent, and the Prince Regent himself. Austen did have some relative success with some of her novels immediately following their publication, while others didn't sell as well:

- *Pride and Prejudice* was her most popular novel, selling out its first edition of 1,000 copies in less than two years.

- The first edition of *Sense and Sensibility* sold out in 1813, after being published in 1811.

- The first edition of *Mansfield Park* sold out in just six months – however the second edition did very badly, meaning that Jane lost a lot of money.

- *Emma* sold 1,248 copies in nine months, but only increased to a mere 1,437 after four years.

- The combined edition of *Northanger Abbey* and *Persuasion* sold 1,409 copies within a year.

Although Jane's novels were popular she didn't make very much money from them, mainly as a result of publishing on commission. Between 1811 and 1817 she made just £630 (about $32,130 now): not a sufficient income for a gentry lady to live on. As a comparison, consider that Jane's dress allowance for one year was £20 ($1,020), and that she had the lowest allowance of her entire family.

GETTING REVIEWED

Sense and Sensibility and *Pride and Prejudice* did receive reviews in some of the journals of the day, such as the *British Critic* and *The Critical Review*. Most of these reviews were short and didn't go into much detail, but they were favorable. Jane's most important review came from Sir Walter Scott when he reviewed *Emma* for *The Quarterly Review*. He used Austen's novel as part of a larger defense of the novel form, and praised her work for its realism. In 1821 Jane received further praise from Whatley, a critic who compared her work with that of Shakespeare and Homer.

JANE'S ENDURING REPUTATION

Going into the Victorian era, Jane's novels lost some of their popularity as they didn't fit the mold expected of a Victorian novel. While the works of writers like Dickens became popular, Austen's work lost its appeal, meaning that there were no new editions printed of her work, although her novels never went out of print.

In 1869 James Edward Austen-Leigh published his *Memoir of Jane Austen*. This work sparked an interest in Jane and her novels saw a rise in new editions, with the first popular and collected editions of her work appearing in 1883.

Pocket Fact 🔱

Although Austen's popularity did fall off slightly during the Victorian age, her novels were translated and published abroad soon after their initial publication. All six of her novels had been published in France by the middle of the 1820s.

This new popularity was scorned by literary critics who wanted to distinguish their appreciation of Austen's work from that of the masses. They coined the term 'Janeite' to describe themselves and this movement saw the beginning of literary criticism of Jane Austen. In 1911 the Oxford scholar Bradley published an essay on Austen's work, marking a new academic appreciation for her novels. In 1923 the first scholarly edition of Austen's novels was published, making it the first scholarly edition of any English writer. Austen's work has seen a continuous growth in its academic reputation since this point.

MODERN INTERPRETATIONS OF JANE AUSTEN

If you type 'Jane Austen' into Amazon you will be met with pages of different editions of Jane's novels. You will also be met by a wide range of modern novels inspired by Jane and her characters. By the year 2000 it was estimated that there were over 100 printed adaptations of her work, ranging from sequels to erotica to horror stories. Most of the spin-offs inspired by Austen's novels stem from *Pride and Prejudice*, and here are just a few notable examples:

- *Pride and Prejudice Continues* (a series of books)

- *Fitzwilliam Darcy, gentleman* (a series of books)

- *Mr Darcy Takes a Wife*

- *The Pemberley Variations*

- *Letters from Pemberley*

Pocket Fact

In 2010 a signed edition of Emma *sold for £325,000 (approx. $522,000) at an auction in England. The novel is signed with a dedication to Jane's friend Anne Sharp, who was governess to Jane's niece Fanny.*

Jane Austen herself has also inspired a number of modern novels, such as:

- *Confessions of a Jane Austen Addict*

- *Talking about Jane Austen in Baghdad*

- *The Jane Austen Book Club*

- *The Lost Memoirs of Jane Austen*

- *A Walk with Jane Austen*

Horror and Jane Austen

Although Jane was praised for her accurate portrayal of real people living through plausible circumstances, in recent years there has been a rapid growth in the number of horror stories inspired by her work. These titles include:

- Mr Darcy, Vampyre
- Jane bites back
- Pride and Prejudice and Zombies
- Sense and Sensibility and Sea Monsters
- Emma and the Werewolves
- Persuasion . . . in Space!

It has also been announced that Elton John's film company is making a film called Pride and Predator*: the story of what happens when aliens invade Longbourn. These adaptations play upon the juxtaposition of Austen's propriety and the lurid pulp quality of some horror archetypes. It seems that the realism of Jane Austen's work is the perfect foil for the outlandish premises of camp horror – a match made in heaven!*

5

'The person, be it gentleman or lady, who has not pleasure in a good novel, must be intolerably stupid': Jane Austen's novels

Just a quick warning: this chapter contains plot spoilers!

◈ SENSE AND SENSIBILITY (1811) ◈

ABOUT THE NOVEL

Sense and Sensibility was Austen's first published novel. Its three volumes appeared in 1811 under the pseudonym 'A Lady'. Austen herself paid for the novel to be published and even had to pay the publisher a commission on the sales. The first edition of the novel had a print run of less than 1,000 copies, all of which had sold out less than two years later. Austen had written an earlier version of *Sense and Sensibility*, titled *Elinor and Marianne*, in letter form.

SYNOPSIS

The novel opens with the death of Mr Dashwood, whose estate, Norland Park, passes to his son from his first marriage, John Dashwood. This leaves the second Mrs Dashwood and her three daughters Elinor, Marianne and Margaret with only a very small income and nowhere to live. John had promised his father that he would care for his half-sisters but his selfish wife, Fanny, convinces him against any financial help. John and Fanny move into Norland Park and, despite the growing attachment between Elinor and

Fanny's brother Edward, the Dashwood women are forced to begin looking for another place to live.

The Dashwood women are invited to move to Barton Cottage on the estate of their cousin Sir John Middleton. There the Dashwood women meet Sir John's mother-in-law Mrs Jennings, as well as his friend, Colonel Brandon, who shows an interest in Marianne but Marianne finds the older man's attentions ridiculous.

One day Marianne is swept off her feet (literally!) by the handsome John Willoughby, who rescues Marianne, carrying her home when she falls and twists her ankle. Marianne is instantly besotted with Willoughby and they become inseparable. Marianne openly displays her feelings and preference for him, despite the whispers of their small society. Elinor suspects they are secretly engaged and tries to warn Marianne against her unreserved behavior but Marianne refuses to hide her feelings.

Suddenly though, Willoughby tells Marianne that his aunt (from whom he is to inherit his estate) is sending him to London and he will not return for at least a year. He leaves immediately, leaving Marianne devastated. At this point Edward finally visits but Elinor is so dismayed at his downcast behavior that she fears that he no longer cares for her, and so hides her own feelings.

Lucy and Anne Steele, cousins of the Middletons, visit, and after Mrs Jennings mentions Edward, Elinor is confronted by Lucy, who confesses that she and Edward have been secretly engaged for four years. Lucy explains that due to her low social standing she and Edward have decided to hide their engagement as his ambitious mother would never consent to the marriage. A shocked Elinor agrees to keep Lucy's secret and hides her despair from her family.

Mrs Jennings invites Marianne and Elinor to spend the winter with her in London where Marianne writes a frantic series of letters to Willoughby, but she receives no response. Worse still, when they meet Willoughby at a ball he snubs Marianne. The next day Willoughby writes to Marianne, returning all her letters and her lock of hair, and informing her that he is now engaged to a Miss Grey. Marianne is devastated and finally confesses to Elinor that she and Willoughby were never truly engaged but that she believed he loved her.

Colonel Brandon visits Elinor and relates the sad tale of his former love, Eliza Williams, who was forced to marry his brother, and after this marriage ended badly fell so low in society that when the Colonel eventually found her, she was dying of consumption in a poor house. In her final days Eliza entrusted the Colonel with the care of her daughter. After caring for the child for years the Colonel was devastated when she disappeared, and after a frantic search found her alone and pregnant, having been abandoned by her seducer: Willoughby. Elinor decides to relate this new information to Marianne, who is shocked to learn the truth of Willoughby's character.

John and Fanny arrive in London and invite Lucy and Anne Steele to stay. One day Mrs Jennings returns home with the news that Anne has told Fanny of the engagement between Lucy and Edward, and that Fanny was so enraged that she has thrown Lucy out of her house.

Upon learning of his engagement, Mrs Ferrars gives Edward an ultimatum: end the engagement or be disinherited. Edward honorably refuses to abandon Lucy, meaning he is disinherited and his brother Robert receives the inheritance instead. Elinor meets Anne, who tells her that Edward has decided to enter the church, but that he and Lucy will have to wait until he has his own parish to marry. Colonel Brandon, out of admiration for Edward's actions, offers him the parish on his estate, which Edward accepts.

While on their journey home to Barton, Marianne indulges her misery, taking long solitary walks, even walking out in the rain at night. She catches a cold and soon becomes very ill. Colonel Brandon goes to fetch Mrs Dashwood and, hearing a carriage, Elinor rushes to meet it. She is then shocked when Willoughby enters. Elinor asks him to leave but he begs to be allowed to explain his actions in the hope that she and Marianne may forgive him, and so Elinor agrees to listen.

Willoughby confesses that he had decided to propose to Marianne when his aunt found out about his conduct with Colonel Brandon's ward. Willoughby refused to marry Eliza and so was cut off.

Willoughby went to London and soon entered into an engagement with the wealthy Miss Grey. He explains that Miss Grey forced him to snub Marianne at the party and that she dictated his response to Marianne's final letter. When Willoughby learned that Marianne was dying he immediately rushed to see her, as he was unable to bear the thought of her dying while hating him. Elinor pities Willoughby and agrees to relate his confession to Marianne. The Dashwoods return to Barton Cottage and Marianne slowly grows better, stating that she will now devote her life to quiet study. One day Elinor relates Willoughby's tale to Marianne, who realizes that she would not have had a happy marriage with Willoughby.

Soon after the Dashwood women are told by one of their servants that he has met 'Mrs Ferrars'. Elinor is hurt but bears the news well. Soon after this Elinor sees a gentleman approach the cottage and is shocked to see it is Edward. Edward arrives and Mrs Dashwood inquires after 'Mrs Ferrars' to which Edward replies that his mother is well. Mrs Dashwood says that she meant 'Mrs Edward Ferrars' and Edward corrects her, saying she must mean 'Mrs Robert Ferrars'. The women are utterly astonished as Edward relates that Lucy has in fact married his brother Robert. Edward then proposes to Elinor, and although he is loath to apologise for acting honorably he goes to visit his mother and she gives her consent to the marriage, giving Edward an income which will support them. Edward and Elinor are soon married and move to the parsonage at Delaford.

Mrs Dashwood, Marianne and Margaret are frequent visitors at Delaford, where Marianne, who has now matured beyond her youthful fancies about marriage, realizes the good match she makes with the Colonel and they are also married. Mrs Dashwood is thrilled that her two daughters are happy, and Margaret, who is now old enough for dancing, becomes the focus of Sir John and Lady Middleton's schemes.

MAIN THEMES TO WATCH OUT FOR

Sense *vs.* sensibility

Obviously the dichotomy between feelings of 'sense' and feelings of 'sensibility', and the behavior arising from these feelings, constitutes a major theme in this novel. In portraying the experiences of her characters, Austen plays out the battle that occurs in all of us between sense and sensibility, or logic and our emotions, and the necessity of learning to balance these extremes. It is worth pointing out though that Elinor does not solely display sense while Marianne only displays sensibility; both sisters have a mixture of each feeling, illustrating that it is essential to find a balance between the two, rather than blindly following one extreme.

Honorable intentions

In comparing the behavior and values embodied by Edward and Willoughby we are presented with an exploration of honorable behavior, and what should be done to both preserve our duty and act according to our passions. Edward and Willoughby begin with the same circumstances: they are both set to inherit a comfortable lifestyle but only at the whim of a relative. While Edward lives a careful life, concealing an engagement to protect his family, Willoughby acts selfishly, leaving Eliza Williams pregnant and alone. When their respective families find out about their romantic entanglements, Edward does the honorable thing and stands by Lucy even though he loses his inheritance. Willoughby on the other hand refuses to marry Eliza and loses his inheritance as a result. By the end of the novel we see that Edward has been rewarded for his honorable behavior by marrying a woman who truly cares for him. Willoughby on the other hand has entered into a loveless marriage, only to real-ize that if he had behaved in an honorable fashion he could have mar-ried Marianne AND received his inheritance.

Pocket Fact 🔱

In 2009 the second 'mash-up' novel by publisher Quirk was released: Sense and Sensibility and Sea Monsters. *In this alternative version of the classic tale, the Dashwood sisters are exiled to a strange island, where the creatures of the sea have turned against humanity. The same romantic twists and turns take place and the novel has largely the same conclusion, although Marianne now objects to both Colonel Brandon's age and the fact that he is a half-man, half-squid.*

Austen's Juvenilia

As a child Jane Austen wrote frequently, experimenting with the comic forms that would permeate her later novels and the writing she did between 1787 and 1793 (between the ages of 11 and 18) is generally known as her Juvenilia. *She copied many of her stories into a set of notebooks her father bought her, inside of which he had written, 'Effusions of Fancy by a very young lady consisting of tales in a style entirely new'.*

Austen divided her youthful scribbling into three volumes:

- Volume the First *contains her early attempts at novels, such as* Jack and Alice *and* Henry and Eliza.
- Volume the Second *contains Austen's burlesque work* Love and Freindship (sic) *and* A History of England, *her parody of Oliver Goldsmith's work.*
- Volume the Third *contains* Catharine *and* Evelyn.

Many of these early works contain comic scenes of violence and drunkenness, perhaps written mainly for the entertainment of her brothers, and it is obvious how Austen honed her humorous tone. Although these early writings differ greatly from Austen's well known novels, they can provide an interesting insight into Austen's early attempts at becoming the writer we know and love.

 PRIDE AND PREJUDICE (1813)

ABOUT THE NOVEL

Austen began *Pride and Prejudice* in 1796 – then titled *First Impressions* – her first serious effort at producing a manuscript for publication. Like *Sense and Sensibility* this novel is a comedy of manners, revolving around opposing manners and morals, which guide the characters through the pitfalls of inheritance and marriage. The first edition of the novel was published in 1813 and thanks to good reviews quickly sold out, meaning a second edition was published later that year.

SYNOPSIS

The novel opens with Mrs Bennet who, on hearing that the wealthy Mr Bingley has moved into the nearby estate Netherfield Park, decides he should marry one of her five daughters. Her plan progresses well when Mr Bingley dances twice with her eldest daughter Jane, but her second daughter Elizabeth is slighted by Bingley's friend, the wealthy but haughty Mr Darcy.

Despite dismissing Elizabeth, Darcy begins to admire her: a growing attachment Elizabeth remains unaware of. A regiment of militia then arrive in Meryton – a great excitement for the younger Bennet girls. Jane is invited to dine at Netherfield and when Mrs Bennet makes her ride there in the rain, she catches a cold and is forced to stay. Elizabeth is concerned for her sister and walks the three miles to see her. Bingley's sisters are shocked at her appearance when she arrives, but her actions only increase Darcy's admiration. Elizabeth is invited to stay at Netherfield as well, and she and Darcy engage in a series of witty exchanges which increase his love for her.

Jane recovers, and she and Elizabeth return to Longbourn, just in time to welcome their cousin Mr Collins. Mr Collins will inherit Longbourn when Mr Bennet dies and he has come to find a wife among his cousins. Mrs Bennet encourages Mr Collins' scheme, suggesting he focus his attentions on Elizabeth.

One day Elizabeth meets Mr Wickham, a pleasing young man who has just joined the militia, and he tells Elizabeth the sad story of his past. It seems Wickham was meant to receive a parsonage from Darcy's father but when he died the young Darcy gave the living to someone else, leaving Wickham destitute. Elizabeth's dislike of Darcy is now greatly increased.

Mr Bingley holds a ball at Netherfield, where Elizabeth reluctantly accepts Darcy's invitation to dance, during which they argue about Wickham. Despite this, Elizabeth is happy to see how much Bingley admires her sister, although she is mortified at the embarrassing behavior of her family.

The next day proves no better for Elizabeth as Mr Collins makes her an offer of marriage. Elizabeth bluntly refuses him, despite the repeated entreaties of her mother. Mrs Bennet hopes she may be able to push one of her other daughters on Mr Collins but her hopes are dashed when the Bennet's neighbor, Charlotte Lucas, flatters Mr Collins enough to convince him to propose to her.

Jane receives a letter from Miss Bingley explaining that the Bingleys have gone to London, with no intention of returning to Netherfield that year. Jane is hurt at the news and Elizabeth sees that Bingley has been taken to London to separate him from Jane. Mrs Bennet's brother and his wife arrive, and invite Jane to stay with them in London, in the hope that it may bring her and Bingley together again, but while she is there Jane doesn't meet with Bingley. Elizabeth also suffers a slight when she sees Wickham transferring his attentions to another young woman, but realizes that she was not in love with him.

Elizabeth goes to visit the newly married Charlotte and soon after her arrival she is invited to wait on Lady Catherine de Bourgh, Mr Collins' patroness. Elizabeth is forced to listen to Lady Catherine's constant advice and opinions on every subject, and then is forced to meet with Darcy who has come to visit Lady Catherine, his aunt. Elizabeth and Darcy continue the same kind of witty exchange they had at Netherfield, and she grows increasingly puzzled when he keeps visiting her at the Parsonage. Elizabeth is then shocked when Darcy's cousin reveals that Darcy has purposefully concealed Jane's presence in London from Bingley.

One day Elizabeth is alone when Darcy enters and suddenly declares that he loves her. Elizabeth is utterly shocked and is soon offended as Darcy goes on to declare his feelings, despite the inferiority and ill behavior of her family. She refuses him and goes on to describe that she has several reasons to think badly of him, not least his treatment of her sister and Wickham. He promptly leaves the house, but the next morning gives Elizabeth a letter in which he tries to defend himself. He explains that he separated

Jane and Bingley mainly from the belief that Jane was indifferent to Bingley, but he did consider her a poor match. Darcy then relates that Wickham had actually refused the promised living, asking for the pecuniary equivalent instead. When Darcy refused to give Wickham the living once he had spent all of this money, Wickham seduced Darcy's 15 year old sister, Georgiana, to gain access to her inheritance. Darcy managed to prevent their elopement and Wickham fled, leaving Georgiana heartbroken.

After reading the letter Elizabeth is ashamed of the prejudice she has shown towards Darcy and begins to regret the manner in which she refused his offer. Elizabeth returns home and while she is pleased to learn the militia are leaving, she is dismayed to find out that Lydia has been invited to accompany one of the officer's wives. She begs her father to prevent the trip but he refuses.

Elizabeth goes on a trip with her aunt and uncle to Derbyshire, and while there they propose a visit to Pemberley, Darcy's estate. Elizabeth finds out Darcy is away from home and so agrees to go. At Pemberley Elizabeth is overcome by the beauty of the grounds and the house. As they enter the garden though they are suddenly met by Darcy himself. Darcy manages to recover his shock but Elizabeth is utterly mortified, and then amazed at his being civil to her. She is further shocked when he accompanies her on a walk and is pleasant to her aunt and uncle.

A few days later Elizabeth receives a letter from Jane, which reveals that Lydia has run away with Wickham. While Elizabeth is reading, Darcy enters and she tells him what has happened. On seeing his reaction, and realizing that this scandal will separate them forever, Elizabeth suddenly realizes that she is in love with Darcy.

Elizabeth returns to Longbourn and Mr Gardiner goes to London to help with the search. A few days later he writes stating that Wickham and Lydia have been found but they are not married. Mr Gardiner has negotiated with Wickham and if Mr Bennet agrees to give Lydia her inheritance as well as £100 a year (about $5,100 now), then Wickham will marry her. Mr Bennet agrees but shares his concern with Jane and Elizabeth that their uncle must have paid Wickham almost £10,000 (about $510,000 now), as well as paying off his debts to make him agree to so small an annual payment.

Lydia and Wickham arrive at Longbourn after their marriage and Elizabeth is disgusted to see Lydia boasting of being married before her sisters. Later as she is telling Elizabeth about the wedding, she lets slip that Darcy was there. A shocked Elizabeth then writes to her aunt who reveals that Darcy had been the one to discover Lydia and Wickham's whereabouts and he carried out all the negotiations with Wickham. Elizabeth then realizes that it was Darcy who has paid the £10,000 to make the marriage happen.

Wickham and Lydia leave and the next news is of Bingley's return to Netherfield. Bingley arrives at Longbourn, bringing Darcy with him. Elizabeth is mortified by her mother's warm reception of Bingley compared to her cold greeting to Darcy. Despite this though Elizabeth is pleased to see that Bingley is still in love with Jane. Mrs Bennet's efforts are finally paid off when Bingley proposes to Jane. The family are delighted and Mrs Bennet is overjoyed at the thought of her daughter being married to such a wealthy gentleman.

Soon after Lady Catherine de Bourgh unexpectedly arrives at the house and asks Elizabeth to walk with her. When they are alone Lady Catherine reveals that she has heard Darcy and Elizabeth are engaged and has come to hear Elizabeth deny it. Elizabeth reveals they are not engaged but will not promise never to enter into an engagement with Darcy, meaning Lady Catherine angrily leaves. Although this news allows Elizabeth to hope, she worries that Darcy will be unable to ignore his aunt's arguments.

Darcy arrives a few days later, and Elizabeth, finding herself alone with him, thanks him for his assistance with Lydia. He accepts her thanks but tells her he acted only for her. He confesses he still loves her and says Elizabeth's encounter with his aunt allowed him to hope. They both realize that their love for each other has inspired them to amend their poor behavior. That evening Elizabeth's family are shocked at her engagement, but on realizing that Elizabeth truly loves Darcy they are overjoyed. Elizabeth and Darcy are soon married and move to Pemberley.

MAIN THEMES TO WATCH OUT FOR

Interplay of pride and prejudice

Throughout the novel, Austen uses the feelings and behaviors of Darcy and Elizabeth to drive the action and to outline the interplay between the two eponymous morals explored in this novel: pride and prejudice. Austen uses Darcy's pride and Elizabeth's prejudice against him to develop their relationship. Although these respective feelings prevent their being together for most of the novel, by being forced to confront their failings they become better people and ultimately end up happy together.

Marriage, wealth and inheritance

Mrs Bennet's determination to see her daughters married outlines the importance of marriage, and its connection to wealth and inheritance. Mr Bennet's daughters cannot inherit their father's property and so must marry well to secure their future. The sense of duty to her family that is attached to a young woman's marriage is explored in this novel in the proposals made by Mr Collins. Elizabeth refuses his offer, despite her mother's entreaties that she will save her family if she accepts him. Charlotte Lucas on the other hand is quick to seize the opportunity and does her 'duty' by encouraging Mr Collins and securing her place as his wife. The happiness of her family in her marriage, arising equally from their relief that she will not be a financial burden to her brothers as much as their pleasure that she will eventually be mistress of Longbourn, highlights just how intrinsically marriage and wealth were linked.

Pocket Fact ♆

In 2003 Pride and Prejudice *was voted into second place in the BBC's poll of the UK's Best-Loved Book, beaten only by* The Lord of the Rings. *In 2008 in Australia* Pride and Prejudice *topped a list of the 101 Best Books Ever Written.*

Lady Susan

Between 1794 and 1795 Austen began work on an ambitious project entitled Lady Susan. *This work is written entirely in letters, a style Austen would also use and then edit out in* Sense and Sensibility *and* Pride and Prejudice. *The title character is an older woman, a widow who uses her charm and beauty to manipulate everyone around her. Lady Susan cares only for herself and despite her cruel treatment of her daughter and sister-in-law, she is a fascinating character. Austen finally completed the untitled work in 1803 but she never sought to publish it. The story was eventually given a title and published by Jane's nephew, James Edward Austen-Leigh, as part of his* Memoir of Jane Austen *in 1871.*

✿ MANSFIELD PARK (1814) ✿

ABOUT THE NOVEL

Mansfield Park was Austen's third published novel, written between 1812 and 1814 and published in 1814. The publication of this novel differs from Austen's earlier publications in that it is Austen's first novel that was not a revision of an earlier work. The Austen who wrote *Mansfield Park* was older and more mature and this shows in the pragmatic, less romantic content of the novel.

Mansfield Park is one of Austen's less popular novels, although it was praised upon its publication for its morality. One reason this novel does not rank as highly with readers is because many (Austen's own mother included!) cannot warm to the heroine, Fanny Price. The novel is not so much about Fanny's romantic journey as her observation of the romance occurring around her, with Fanny pining for a man who doesn't return her love until the final pages, meaning some readers find the passive Fanny hard to engage with.

SYNOPSIS

Mansfield Park opens with the marriages of the Ward sisters: Miss Maria marries Sir Thomas Bertram of Mansfield Park; Miss Ward marries a reverend, while Miss Frances defies her family and marries a poor sailor, becoming only Mrs Price. All communication ceases between the sisters for some time until Mrs Price writes asking for help to support her large family. Mrs Norris suggests that they invite their niece Fanny to live at Mansfield Park. Sir Thomas agrees but states that the child must be treated differently to his own children. Fanny Price arrives, a shy, frightened child who is teased by her cousins for her lack of education and poor background and used as a servant by her aunt Norris. Only her cousin Edmund is kind to her.

Mr Norris dies, but rather than going to Edmund as was the original plan, Sir Thomas is forced to give the parish living on the estate to a Dr Grant, to pay off his son Tom's debts. Dr Grant arrives with his wife and they settle at the parsonage. Sir Thomas then leaves for Antigua, to oversee his business there. While he is away Mrs Norris orchestrates an engagement between Maria and the wealthy Mr Rushworth. Sir Thomas approves the match, but the wedding is postponed until his return. At this time the half brother and sister of Mrs Grant – Henry and Mary Crawford, both wealthy, lively people – arrive at Mansfield.

Henry and Mary's charms soon win the Bertram family over. Despite Maria's engagement the flirtatious Henry focuses his attentions on her, while Mary is forced to admit Edmund's charms, even though he is the younger son and will not inherit the estate. Edmund is similarly charmed with Mary but is blind to her obvious faults. Mary and Edmund argue when she learns that he is to become a clergyman, but despite this Fanny is forced to witness Edmund's growing preference for Mary.

A letter arrives saying Sir Thomas will return soon and Maria begins to dread her impending marriage. Fanny is disgusted by Henry's behavior with her cousins although Edmund fails to see it. Tom has a friend to visit, a Mr Yates, whose stories of acting inspire the group to put on a play. Edmund and Fanny are both horrified at the impropriety of the scheme, but Edmund relents and even agrees to take a part. The whole household is consumed by the play, except Fanny who steadfastly refuses to take a part, and who is instead forced to watch Edmund and Mary rehearse a romantic scene.

On the evening of the dress rehearsal, Sir Thomas unexpectedly returns and the play has to be abandoned. Sir Thomas is furious at what has gone on in his absence, but he is pleased by the improvement in Fanny's looks. Maria hopes that Henry will now declare his love for her, but she is disappointed when he leaves. Out of spite Maria agrees to go ahead with the wedding, even after her father voices his concerns. She and Mr Rushworth are married and go on their honeymoon, taking Julia with them.

Edmund and Mary continue to argue over his choice of career meaning their relationship does not advance. Henry returns and seeing Fanny's dislike of him, cruelly decides to make Fanny fall in love with him, but when he observes her during her brother William's visit he begins to genuinely care for her. Sir Thomas notices Henry's regard and decides to hold a ball for Fanny. At the ball Fanny is embarrassed when Henry asks her to dance but is thankful that he is taking William to meet his uncle, an Admiral, who can help further William's naval career.

Edmund leaves to prepare for his ordination and Henry soon returns to tell Fanny that William has been made a lieutenant. Fanny is thrilled but is wary of the attention Henry is paying to her. When Henry declares his feelings for her she cannot believe he is serious. The next day Sir Thomas tells Fanny that Henry has asked for her hand. He is shocked by Fanny's refusal and grows angry with her, pointing out what a good prospect this is for a woman with no fortune or social standing but Fanny still refuses.

Sir Thomas now proposes that Fanny return home to Portsmouth, thinking that the visit will convince her of her real poverty and to accept Henry. Fanny is pleased at the thought of seeing her real family, but on arriving is shocked at just how small and dirty her family home is. She receives only a lukewarm reception from her parents and her brothers and sisters are loud and uneducated. Only her sister Susan offers Fanny any kind of companionship.

Fanny is surprised when Henry unexpectedly visits but she is impressed by the great improvement in his manners and opinions. Soon after this though a letter arrives from Mary telling Fanny to ignore any rumors she may hear about Henry. Fanny is puzzled until her father reads in the paper that Maria has run away with Henry. Fanny is shocked by this news, and the further revelation that Julia has eloped with Mr Yates. Edmund then arrives to take Fanny and Susan back to Mansfield. At Mansfield Edmund tells Fanny that he met with Mary in London, and on learning that she didn't find Henry and Maria's behavior morally repugnant, left intending to never see her again. Edmund pines over Mary, but realizes he was mistaken about her true character.

Sir Thomas suffers from his daughters' conduct, in knowing that he should have checked their behavior more. Maria cannot be convinced to leave Henry and after he cannot be persuaded to marry her their growing resentment forces them to part. Maria is left to live with Mrs Norris in seclusion. Henry meanwhile is left with the knowledge that if he had resisted his vanity he could have won Fanny. Tom recovers from a serious illness and loses his selfish, wild ways, becoming useful to his father. Once Edmund has stopped regretting Mary he soon realizes what a fine woman Fanny is and they are married. After Dr Grant's death Edmund is able to take up the living at Mansfield.

MAIN THEMES TO WATCH OUT FOR

Morality *vs.* having fun

Mansfield Park was praised for its moral examination, exploring as it does the moral dilemmas faced by one household. The arrival of the exciting Crawfords presents a quandary for the young people at Mansfield, as they are faced with the temptation of an exciting lifestyle that goes against the strict morals they have been taught. The novel ends well for Fanny and Edmund, who have managed to stay most true to their moral values, and ends badly for those who followed their desire to have fun, such as Mary and Henry.

Marriage for love *vs.* money

The Crawfords have no respect for marriage, with Henry seducing both Maria and Julia, and even pursuing the married Maria only to abandon her later. Maria Bertram also provides a warning against marrying purely for money, as she ends up married to a man she hates. Both of these characters end up losing the person they love through a combination of their loose morals and their flippant approach to marriage, showing why one should respect marriage and only marry for love.

Pocket Fact 🔱

J K Rowling has admitted that she named Finch's pet cat in the Harry Potter *books after Fanny's horrible aunt Mrs Norris.*

🐚 *EMMA* (1815) 🐚

ABOUT THE NOVEL

Emma was Austen's fourth published novel, and her first to be published by John Murray. The novel appeared in December 1815, after Austen took just 14 months to write the manuscript. *Emma* was the last novel to appear in Austen's lifetime and was Austen's biggest critical success after Sir Walter Scott used the novel as a part of his defense of the novel form in *The Quarterly Review*.

SYNOPSIS

The novel begins with the marriage of Emma Woodhouse's former governess, Miss Taylor. Emma is sad to see her close friend go, but does pride herself on setting up the match, even boasting to her neighbor and brother-in-law Mr Knightley. He warns her not to interfere in other's lives but Emma ignores him and decides to find a match for Mr Elton, the local parson.

Emma becomes friendly with Harriet Smith, a lower class girl with no fortune and a completely unknown background. Emma decides to groom her for the higher levels of society, beginning by trying to destroy Harriet's regard for Robert Martin, a local farmer.

Emma then begins trying to match Harriet with Mr Elton, and when Mr Elton begs to be allowed to frame a portrait of Harriet that Emma has drawn, Emma decides she has succeeded.

Soon after this, Harriet announces to Emma that she has received a proposal from Mr Martin. Emma is alarmed but after some careful manipulation convinces Harriet to refuse the offer. When Mr Knightley learns what Emma has done he is furious, and tells Emma not to give Harriet ideas above her station, also saying that Mr Elton will want to marry a richer woman. Emma is affected by the truth of his words but chooses to ignore him.

Emma and Harriet begin to compile a book of riddles, and when they ask Mr Elton for help, he gives them a riddle that spells 'courtship'. Emma takes this as further proof of Mr Elton's love for Harriet but at the Weston's Christmas party she is disturbed by how much attention Mr Elton pays to her. Emma's fears are realized when on their carriage ride home Mr Elton declares his love for her. In mentioning Harriet Mr Elton reveals how insulting this is to him, and when Emma steadfastly refuses him he angrily leaves. Emma is now forced to face the fact that she has been mistaken and that she will have to tell Harriet what has happened. Emma breaks the news to Harriet and is pleased when she learns Mr Elton has gone to Bath.

Emma goes to visit her neighbor, the overly talkative Miss Bates, and learns her niece Jane Fairfax is coming to visit. Jane has been living with her adoptive family the Campbells, but she has come to stay with her aunt and grandmother before she begins her career as a governess.

News arrives that Mr Elton is going to be married and Emma worries about the impact on Harriet, but she is distracted by the long awaited arrival of Frank Churchill, Mr Weston's son from his first marriage. Everyone finds Frank a pleasant, handsome young man and Frank amuses Emma by postulating that Mr Dixon, Miss Campbell's new husband, is actually in love with Jane, and when a pianoforte is sent to Jane by an unknown sender Frank guesses it is from Mr Dixon.

Frank becomes consumed with organizing a ball and Emma is pleased when Frank asks her for the first two dances.

When Frank's aunt falls ill though he has to leave and the ball is postponed. On saying goodbye Emma thinks that his manner means he is in love with her, but on reflection she realizes that she does not love Frank. She is suddenly struck by the idea of a match between Frank and Harriet though.

Mr Elton arrives with his bride, whom Emma is disappointed to find is a crass woman, obsessed with her newly made fortune. Frank then returns and a date is decided for the ball, where Emma enjoys their dance but is puzzled by Frank's odd behavior. Emma is thrilled to see Mr Knightley lead Harriet to the dance floor after she has been cruelly snubbed by Mr Elton. The next day though Frank arrives with a very distressed Harriet, whom he has just rescued from an attack by some gypsies in the woods. Once Harriet has recovered, she burns the silly treasures which reminded her of Mr Elton. She then tells Emma of her admiration for a new man and Emma, determined not to get involved, won't allow her to name Frank but says she approves of Harriet's choice.

While all of Highbury thinks Frank has designs on Emma, Mr Knightley begins to suspect a relationship between Frank and Jane. Emma laughs off this idea though, which Mr Knightley takes as proof of an agreement between her and Frank. On an outing to Box Hill, Emma is very rude to Miss Bates during a word game Frank has suggested and on their leaving Mr Knightley criticizes Emma harshly for her behavior. The next day she goes to visit Miss Bates to apologize but doesn't get to see Jane whom she is told is very ill. Emma also learns that Jane has just agreed to accept a governess position.

Emma meets Mr Knightley who tells her he is going to London, and Emma is relieved that he approves of her going to visit Miss Bates. Emma is then invited to visit Mrs Weston, whom she rushes to, worried at the grave manner of the invitation. Mrs Weston tells Emma the shocking news that Frank's aunt has died, and that he has revealed that he and Jane have been secretly engaged for months. Emma assuages the Weston's worries by assuring them she does not love Frank but she is still critical of Jane and Frank's behavior.

Emma begins to worry about Harriet's reaction but on meeting with her, finds her remarkably calm. Emma is then shocked to realize that Harriet is actually in love with Mr Knightley. Emma begins to try to understand why she is so upset by Harriet's being in love with Mr Knightley. Suddenly Emma realizes that **she** is in love with Mr Knightley.

Realizing that she has always cared for Mr Knightley Emma is now horrified by the idea of a match between him and Harriet. She begins to regret giving Harriet ideas above her station and she begins to panic when she remembers his disappointment in her own behavior recently. Emma awaits his return anxiously, and on meeting with him is afraid he will confess his feelings for Harriet. When he tells Emma that she will soon get over Frank she assures him that she does not care for Frank and Mr Knightley unexpectedly takes this opportunity to tell Emma that he loves her. He tells her that he went to London to escape her relationship with Frank but on hearing of Frank's engagement, left immediately and rode through the rain to return. He returned to comfort her but happily finds the moment to make Emma his own.

Emma is ecstatic; her only unhappiness being the thought that while her father lives she cannot marry Mr Knightley. She also worries about having to tell Harriet and so asks her sister to invite Harriet to London. Emma's first concern is overcome when Mr Knightley kindly offers to move to Hartfield so he and Emma may marry without leaving her father alone. Emma is anxiously awaiting Harriet's return when Mr Knightley tells her that Harriet has entered into an engagement with Robert Martin. Emma realizes that despite all her efforts Harriet has always really been in love with Robert Martin. Soon after, with Mr Woodhouse's approval, Emma and Mr Knightley marry and their friends and family wish them every happiness.

Clues to Frank and Jane's relationship to watch out for on a second reading

- *Frank going to buy gloves to avoid telling Emma about his first meeting with Jane.*

- *When Frank goes to London he doesn't get his haircut but buys the pianoforte for Jane.*
- *Jane walks to the post office without fail to get her letters from Frank, and is even seen going in the rain by John Knightley.*
- *Frank is keen to arrange the ball so he can dance with Jane.*
- *Frank's selfish behavior, flirting with Emma at Box Hill, is what spurs Jane to finally accept a governess position.*

MAIN THEMES TO WATCH OUT FOR

Rank in society

The small Highbury society of *Emma* provides a good example of the different class levels in Austen's time and how these classes behaved and interacted. We see the impact of a person's class in Emma's dismissal of Robert Martin; in the sinking status of Mrs and Miss Bates; and Mr Elton's repulsion at a match between himself and Harriet. *Emma* also provides us with some of the best examples of what it meant to be a gentleman. Mr Knightley's behavior and mode of living throughout the novel can be taken as the pinnacle of what it was to be a Regency gentleman: from his advisory role as a landowner, to his superior way of walking and dancing at the Crown Inn ball.

Career as a governess

Emma is Austen's only novel that thoroughly explores the life and state of a governess. We are offered extreme examples of this career, open to women of genteel breeding who do not have the money or opportunity to marry. Miss Taylor leads the life of a charmed governess, becoming friends with her charge and remaining as a beloved friend in the house until she marries Mr Weston. Despite her good fortune though, Austen uses Mrs Elton to remind us of the stigma of Mrs Weston's background, when she comments on how surprised she was to find Mrs Weston so well mannered. Jane Fairfax's situation provides a stark contrast to Miss Taylor's. She is being forced into her situation through impending poverty, and even likens the search for a governess position to the slave trade.

❦ *NORTHANGER ABBEY* (1817) ❦

ABOUT THE NOVEL

Northanger Abbey is perhaps Austen's most satirical and humorous novel. It was originally written as *Susan* and is considered to be her earliest completed novel. The tone of the novel is therefore closer to the sarcastic, cutting wit of Austen's *Juvenilia* than any of her others. *Northanger Abbey* was eventually published after Jane's death, in a combined edition with *Persuasion*, and it was her brother Henry who prepared the manuscript for print and changed the title to *Northanger Abbey*.

SYNOPSIS

Catherine Morland embarks on her first adventure as a heroine at the age of 17 when her neighbors, the Allens, invite her to Bath. At her first ball in Bath Catherine longs to join in the dancing, but their lack of acquaintance means she cannot, a fact Mrs Allen repeatedly bemoans.

This lonely situation continues until the master of ceremonies approaches one evening and introduces a young man called Henry Tilney. He is handsome and well mannered and asks Catherine to dance. Henry and Catherine dance and talk and when the ball ends Catherine hopes very much to see him again.

The next day Catherine rushes to the Pump Room in the hope of seeing Henry but she is disappointed to find he is not there. Mrs Allen is lucky enough to meet with an old school friend though. Mrs Thorpe introduces her three daughters, and Catherine instantly befriends the eldest, Isabella. Over the next few days the girls become increasingly close, always walking arm in arm and reading novels together. Catherine is in awe of the elder Isabella and her stories of balls and her flirtations with men.

One day Isabella and Catherine unexpectedly meet John, Isabella's brother, and James, Catherine's brother. The brothers and sisters have a happy reunion but when Catherine is left to walk with John she is forced to endure his excessive talk about his gig (a horse and carriage, see glossary), and after his dismissal of her beloved novels, she is left with a poor opinion of him.

That evening Isabella dances with James, leaving Catherine alone as her partner, John, has gone to the card room. Catherine is annoyed to be sitting down, but her feelings change dramatically when she sees Henry coming towards her. She is disappointed when she has to refuse his offer to dance, since she has promised John, but while she is dancing with John she is introduced to Eleanor Tilney, Henry's sister.

The next day Catherine goes to the Pump Room hoping to see Miss Tilney and become better acquainted with her. While she is still at home though John and James appear in their carriages to go for a ride with her and Isabella. Catherine once more finds John disagreeable as he asks about Mr Allen's fortune, and on their return is disappointed to find it is too late to go to the Pump Rooms (see glossary).

The next morning Catherine manages to go to the Pump Rooms and there meets Eleanor. They have a pleasant conversation and Eleanor tells Catherine she and Henry will be at the ball the next evening. After agonizing over her dress Catherine arrives at the ball and is thrilled when Henry asks her to dance again. It is then decided that Henry, Eleanor and Catherine will go for a walk the next day.

The next day the rain prevents Henry and Eleanor coming, but when the sun comes out John arrives claiming Catherine for a drive to Bristol. Catherine says she can't go but when John tells her he has seen Henry and Eleanor leaving town, she agrees. As they set off though Catherine sees Henry and Eleanor walking towards her house, and she is extremely angry that John has lied to her and that he won't stop the carriage to let her out.

The next day Catherine is eager to make things right and so she sets off for the Tilney's house. A servant takes her name but says Eleanor has just gone out. Catherine is then upset to see Eleanor and her father leave the house a few moments later. She is sure she has offended them but at the theater she is thrilled when Henry comes over to her and explains that Eleanor was sorry to refuse

Catherine earlier but was told to do so by her father, who was in a hurry to leave.

The next day the trip to Bristol is proposed again but Catherine refuses as she has rearranged her walk with the Tilneys. She is furious when she finds out John has approached Eleanor and postponed the walk, and rushing after Eleanor she enters the Tilney's house, making copious apologies as she bursts in. The misunderstanding is soon cleared up and Catherine is introduced to General Tilney who greets her very cordially.

The next morning Catherine goes on her walk with Eleanor and Henry where they enter into a lengthy discussion on novels. Catherine goes to visit Isabella the next day and it quickly emerges that Isabella and James are engaged. A letter arrives from James outlining that Mr Morland has agreed to give him and Isabella £400 a year (about $20,400 now). James is satisfied but Catherine is hurt when Isabella and Mrs Thorpe openly discuss how small an amount this is. Later at the Pump Rooms though Catherine is further disappointed in Isabella when she sees her openly flirting with Captain Frederick Tilney, Henry's brother.

Catherine is distracted from the engagement though when Eleanor asks her to come stay at her family home, Northanger Abbey. Catherine is thrilled by the invitation and by the Gothic images aroused by the Abbey. They soon depart for Northanger Abbey and Catherine is delighted when she gets to ride with Henry part of the way. Henry teases her by telling her ghost stories about the Abbey, which Catherine naively believes but on arriving she is disappointed by its modern appearance. Despite this though Catherine cannot help but give in to her Gothic sensibilities and suffers a series of embarrassments, once when she is caught by a maid examining a chest, and later when she scares herself half to death after searching through a cabinet and discovering a mysterious piece of paper, which turns out to be merely a laundry list.

Henry departs for his house at Woodston and Eleanor and the General give Catherine a tour of the Abbey. Eleanor shows Catherine round the gardens and on learning more about the late Mrs Tilney, Catherine gives in to her Gothic notions once more, imagining that the General could have killed his wife, or could even be keeping her prisoner. When Henry later catches Catherine examining his mother's rooms Catherine then confesses her suspicions and Henry criticizes her for giving in to the ridiculous notions from her novels. Catherine is embarrassed and is determined to act sensibly in the future.

Catherine begins to worry that she has heard nothing from Isabella, when a letter from James arrives. In it James tells her the engagement with Isabella is off, and says he hopes her visit at Northanger will be over before Captain Tilney makes his engagement known. Catherine tells Henry and Eleanor what has happened, and they are both shocked but suspect their brother will not return home as the General will not approve the match due to Isabella's lack of fortune. This makes Catherine worry for her chances with Henry, but she comforts herself with the kind treatment the General has shown her.

The General proposes a trip to Woodston and on arriving Catherine is thrilled by the small village and the Parsonage. Henry is there to greet them and on entering the house she is pleased by it. The General claims it only needs a lady's touch and on their way home Catherine is pleased by the General's insinuations and only wishes she knew as much about Henry's desires.

The next day Catherine is shocked to receive a letter from Isabella, in which Isabella adopts her normal tone but does say that she is uneasy about James who has not written to her since he left for Oxford. Catherine doesn't believe Isabella's claims that she truly loves James and decides to not even answer the letter.

Catherine is thrilled when Eleanor asks her to extend her stay but soon after this the two girls are alone in the house when they hear a carriage arriving. Catherine goes to her room and some time later Eleanor appears looking pale and agitated. Eleanor reluctantly tells Catherine that her father has returned and that they have to go visit some other friends, meaning Catherine has to leave the next morning. Catherine is disturbed by this turn of events, but is still more upset when Eleanor says she will not be allowed to visit or even receive letters from Catherine.

After a wretched night, Catherine leaves the house, mortified at the way she has been thrown out, with no servant, and only money from Eleanor to pay for her journey. Catherine is very upset, desperately trying to think how she has offended the General. She also begins to wonder what Henry will think when he finds her gone. After a long journey Catherine finds herself entering Fullerton, and while she is happy to see her family, she is still devastated by the way her trip has ended.

Catherine mopes about and just as her mother begins to think she has been spoiled by Bath a young gentleman arrives at the house who introduces himself as Henry Tilney. Henry soon declares his love for Catherine and explains that Catherine's only offense to the General had been that she was not as rich as he thought she was. Henry explains that the General had been kind to her after John Thorpe had misled him about how rich Catherine was. Henry tells Catherine that he argued with his father when he learned he had thrown Catherine out, and that he nobly stood by her. Henry soon applies to the Morlands for permission to marry their daughter and although they want to give their consent, they say they cannot while the General won't. Luckily for Catherine and Henry though, Eleanor marries a Viscount, which pleases the General so much that he decides to give his consent to Henry and Catherine. Catherine and Henry are then married, just under a year after their first meeting.

Pocket Fact 🔱

During Austen's time it was customary to leave calling cards whenever you visited an acquaintance. The cards were displayed on a dish in the hallway of the house, meaning that other guests could see the important callers. We see calling cards in Austen's novels when Catherine has no card to leave for Eleanor Tilney, and when Elizabeth Elliot proudly displays Lady Dalrymple's card in her hallway.

MAIN THEMES TO WATCH OUT FOR

The tricky art of making friends

The experience of Catherine and Mrs Allen trying to make friends in Bath, proves just how rigorous the social customs of Regency society were. The image of Catherine and Mrs Allen not able to even speak to the people they are sharing a table with is one that seems completely alien to modern readers, but provides a fascinating look into life at that time.

The place of novels

Northanger Abbey is Austen's most self-aware novel in that a major theme of the novel, and driver of action, are novels themselves. Austen uses Catherine's reading of Gothic novels to explore both the merits and flaws of her chosen form, providing both a defense in the words of Henry Tilney, and a warning against confusing fiction and reality. We see Catherine expose herself to embarrassment and ridicule by foolishly thinking the outlandish events of her favorite Gothic novels could actually happen.

Dates of composition vs. dates of publication

Jane Austen revised each of her novels several times before their publication, even extensively changing the format of Sense and Sensibility *and* Pride and Prejudice. *Below you can see just how long these masterpieces took to be published:*

- Sense and Sensibility
  - *Date of first composition: 1795*
  - *Date of publication: 1811*
  - *16 years between first composition and publication*
- Pride and Prejudice
  - *Date of first composition: 1796*
  - *Date of publication: 1813*
  - *17 years between first composition and publication*
- Mansfield Park
  - *Date of first composition: 1812*

○ *Date of publication: 1814*
○ *Two years between first composition and publication*
- Emma
  ○ *Date of first composition: 1814*
  ○ *Date of publication: 1815*
  ○ *One year between first composition and publication*
- Northanger Abbey
  ○ *Date of first composition:1798*
  ○ *Date of publication: 1817*
  ○ *19 years between first composition and publication*
- Persuasion
  ○ *Date of first composition: 1815*
  ○ *Date of publication: 1817*
  ○ *Two years between first composition and publication*

❦ PERSUASION (1817) ❦

ABOUT THE NOVEL

Persuasion is Austen's last completed novel, which she worked on between 1815 and 1816. After completing the work, Austen then completely revised the last two chapters of the novel. *Persuasion* wasn't published until after Austen's death, when it was published in a combined edition with *Northanger Abbey*. Austen had called the manuscript *The Elliots* and it is uncertain who changed the title. *Persuasion* contains praise of the navy and its officers, and also begins to examine the class shift that was occurring in Austen's society, with men rising through the ranks and gaining power based on their achievements and merits, rather than as a result of their rank or name.

SYNOPSIS

The novel opens with Sir Walter Elliot, owner of Kellynch Hall, a vain and proud man, reading his own entry in the Baronetage (a book outlining all of the gentry families in the country). He cares greatly for his eldest daughter Elizabeth, but his daughter Mary only has value as a result of her marriage to a nearby landowner, while his middle daughter Anne is mostly ignored. Lady Elliot had been a sensible woman, but after her death Sir Walter had no check on his extravagant habits and is now deep in debt. He decides to rent out his estate and move to Bath, rather than cut back on any of his spending. Lady Russell, Lady Elliot's close friend, hopes this move will remove Mrs Clay, the daughter of Sir Walter's lawyer, whom she thinks has designs on Sir Walter.

Sir Walter's lawyer manages to find an Admiral Croft to rent Kellynch, whose brother-in-law Mr Wentworth had been a curate in the area. This name causes great agitation in Anne, as it brings back memories of Captain Frederick Wentworth, the brother of Mr Wentworth, whom Anne had been engaged to just over seven years previously. Despite her great love for the Captain, Anne was persuaded to break off the engagement by Lady Russell, due to his lack of rank and fortune. Anne has not seen or heard from the Captain since.

Sir Walter meets with the Admiral and the terms of the lease are agreed. Rather than going to Bath immediately, it is agreed that Anne will visit her sister Mary, and then stay with Lady Russell. Lady Russell is pleased with this scheme; her only disappointment being that Mrs Clay has been asked to go to Bath with Elizabeth. Anne sets off for Uppercross, and after pandering to her sister Mary's selfish needs settles into life there.

Three weeks pass until the day arrives that the Crofts are to move into Kellynch. The Crofts pay a visit and Anne finds Mrs Croft a sensible, open woman, who asks if Anne had heard of her brother's marriage. Anne panics but realizes she means her brother Edward, the curate (a minister), and later on assumes it is also Edward whom the Admiral says will soon be visiting. That evening though she learns it is Captain Wentworth who is coming and she begins to worry about meeting with him again.

Their first meeting is very brief but Anne is mortified when Mary tells her that Captain Wentworth commented that Anne was so changed that he would not have known her again. Anne and Captain Wentworth are frequently in each other's company after this, and she is often hurt by his coldness towards her. The Musgroves listen attentively to all of the Captain's accounts of life in the navy and he is soon the center of attention. Captain Wentworth decides to extend his stay and is soon there every day. Everyone tries to figure out which of the Musgrove girls (Louisa and Henrietta) Captain Wentworth prefers, although Anne knows he is not in love with either girl. One day everyone is out walking when Louisa convinces Henrietta to go to Winthrop where she makes up with Charles Hayter, her cousin who hopes to marry her, leaving Louisa free to win the Captain. Anne overhears a conversation between them in which he praises Louisa's firmness of character, and Anne realizes this is the fault he sees in her.

A few days later Captain Wentworth arrives saying he has found his friend, Captain Harville, living nearby at Lyme. It is then decided that the whole party will go to Lyme. On arriving they are introduced to Captain Harville, his wife, and another naval officer, Captain Benwick. Captain Benwick had been engaged to Harville's sister but she sadly died before he could return from sea. Benwick is very much affected by the loss and has been staying with the Harvilles ever since.

While out walking the next morning, Anne passes a man who looks at her in a very admiring manner, a look which Captain Wentworth notices, and makes Anne aware of the improvement in her looks. On seeing the same gentleman leave the inn, the party inquire and on learning his name realize the man is their cousin Mr William Elliot. Mary is very excited by this but Anne gently reminds her that he has not spoken to their family in years. The party go for a walk and Louisa asks Captain Wentworth to catch her as she jumps down the steps. He says no but she runs up the steps, and jumping a second too early, he misses her and she falls down on the pavement unconscious. The group are dumbstruck with horror, assuming she is dead. Anne has to take charge and tells someone to fetch a doctor. Lousia is then carried to the Harville's house and once inside she opens her eyes but soon falls unconscious again.

The surgeon arrives and says she has a bad concussion but should recover in time. It is decided that Anne, Henrietta and the Captain will return to Uppercross to tell the Musgroves what has happened. They arrive at Uppercross and once the news has been delivered, Captain Wentworth immediately sets off again. The next day news arrives to say Louisa is much the same and the Musgroves decide to go to Lyme as well, while Anne goes to stay with Lady Russell. Charles and Mary return to Uppercross, bringing news that Louisa is beginning to sit up but her nerves are incredibly weak and sensitive. They also say that Captain Wentworth has gone to Portsmouth. Soon after this Anne and Lady Russell set off for Bath, with Anne dreading life in the city. The only news that has reached her recently from them is that Mrs Clay is still staying with them and that Mr Elliot has become reacquainted with his family.

Anne arrives at her father's house in Bath where her father and sister show off their new surroundings, and also tell her all about Mr Elliot and how thrilled they are with him. Anne is suspicious of Mr Elliot's recent reconciliation, and also worries about the growing relationship between Mrs Clay and her father. That evening Mr Elliot arrives, and he soon recognizes Anne from Lyme. As time passes Anne gets to know Mr Elliot better and while she is pleased with his manners, she is still suspicious of his sudden reconciliation. One day the newspaper announces the arrival of the Dowager Viscountess Dalrymple, a very wealthy woman of the nobility who is a cousin of the Elliots. Rather than pander to this 'important' relative though Anne decides to visit an old school friend, a Mrs Smith, who has fallen on hard times. Anne finds a great change in Mrs Smith's appearance but that she is still the same kind-hearted, agreeable person.

Lady Russell has decided that Mr Elliot has a preference for Anne and begins to encourage the match. She tells Anne of her approval and tempts Anne with the fact that the marriage would make her mistress of Kellynch Hall, just like her mother. Anne is tempted by the idea, but soon feels that she still doesn't really know Mr Elliot, and cannot overcome her suspicions.

Anne receives a letter from Mary which tells her Captain Benwick and Louisa are engaged to be married. Anne is shocked but realizes that Benwick and Louisa have fallen in love due to their close situation.

Anne's feelings are then put to the test when she meets with Captain Wentworth unexpectedly. She is with Mr Elliot when she sees Captain Wentworth walking down the street and she only has a few moments to compose herself when he enters the shop she is in. They are both flustered when speaking to each other but on finding out that Anne is to walk home in the rain, the Captain offers her his umbrella. At this moment Mr Elliot comes for Anne and Captain Wentworth remembers him from Lyme, also seeing his admiration for Anne.

A few nights later, Anne attends a concert with her family and the Lady Dalrymple. At the concert Anne sees Captain Wentworth enter and goes to speak to him. While she is speaking to him she is pleased to see her father acknowledge him and on discussing the match between Benwick and Louisa, Anne becomes sure that the Captain still cares for her. Anne is thrilled by this but later has to sit with Mr Elliot and listen to his thinly-veiled advances.

The next morning Anne goes to visit Mrs Smith, and while telling her about the concert Mrs Smith asks if Anne is engaged to Mr Elliot. When Anne assures her she is not, Mrs Smith reveals the shocking truth that it was Mr Elliot who ruined her husband and forced her into debt. She also reveals that Mr Elliot wants to marry Anne to ensure he inherits the title from Sir Walter, and prevent Sir Walter's marriage to Mrs Clay. Anne is deeply shocked by the truth of Mr Elliot's character and cannot believe she was almost persuaded to marry him.

The next day Mary and Charles arrive at the house, relating that they are there with Mrs Musgrove, Henrietta and Captain Harville who have come to prepare for the upcoming weddings of Louisa and Henrietta. Anne goes to visit Mrs Musgrove and the rest of the party and there she meets Captain Wentworth. In talking to him Anne becomes further convinced that he still cares for her, and she is pleased when he is invited to the party her father is hosting.

The next day Anne visits the Musgroves again where once more she is in the company of Captain Wentworth. The Captain begins writing a letter while Anne is discussing the marriage between Louisa and Benwick with Captain Harville. Harville says he is sure that his sister would not have forgotten Benwick so quickly, and he and Anne then enter into a conversation about the difference in the dedication of feelings between the two sexes. Anne argues that while men's feelings may be stronger, women are capable of loving the longest when all hope is gone. Captain Wentworth then rises to leave and Harville goes with him.

Just as quickly as he had left though, Captain Wentworth returns and, looking only at Anne, places a letter on the table. He leaves again and Anne opens the letter to find Captain Wentworth's confession of his continued love for her. He tells her that he will come to the party and her reception of him will tell him her answer. Anne is so overcome by this letter that she cannot hide her feelings from Charles and Mrs Musgrove who think she must be ill. Charles insists on walking home with her and on their way they catch up with Captain Wentworth. Charles leaves Anne with the Captain and by the end of their walk they have renewed their engagement.

Sir Walter makes no objection to the match and it is only Lady Russell who has to acknowledge that she had been wrong about both Captain Wentworth and Mr Elliot. Mr Elliot withdraws to London when he learns of Anne's engagement, and soon sets up Mrs Clay as his mistress there: his new ploy to ensure he receives his title. Anne introduces Captain Wentworth to her friend Mrs Smith and the Captain embraces this friendship, even helping Mrs Smith to reclaim her husband's lost fortune. Anne and Captain Wentworth marry and Anne glories in being a sailor's wife.

Pocket Fact 🔱

In many television adaptations of Persuasion *we see Captain Wentworth, acting for Admiral Croft, asking Anne if she is engaged to Mr Elliot, and whether the Crofts should leave Kellynch. Many readers of* Persuasion *may assume this scene is inserted by the film company, but this scene was in fact Austen's original ending to the novel.*

MAIN THEMES TO WATCH OUT FOR

Changing social world

The dynamic between the sailors and the gentry in *Persuasion* provides readers with a fascinating insight into the shifting class status occurring at this time. While men of the landed gentry are falling into debt and renting out their inherited estates, the men of the navy – with their newly acquired fortunes and social status – are stepping in to rent these houses and take on the positions of power previously held by the gentry. Sir Walter renting out his home to Admiral Croft provides the perfect illustration of this social shift. See p. 22 for more on the changing social classes at this time.

Praise of the navy

The picture Austen paints of the navy in *Persuasion*, the caliber of gentlemen and the camaraderie between the brother officers are some of the highest praise Austen gives to the profession. Austen had two brothers in the navy so she knew first hand what life was like for the sailors and their families, and made sure her portrayal was accurate by checking her facts with her brothers.

❦ AUSTEN'S UNFINISHED WORKS ❦

When Jane died in 1817 she left behind two unfinished works. One was *The Watsons*, a novel she had begun while living in Bath. The story revolves around Emma Watson, a young woman who has returned to her family after living with her wealthy aunt for most of her life. Emma has a sickly father, a poor clergyman, and on returning home finds that she has become accustomed to a much higher lifestyle than her father can provide. Emma is greeted warmly by her sister Elizabeth but is shocked to hear of the bad behavior of her other sisters. Emma also meets with her brother and his rich wife and is forced to realize how low her station has sunk. Emma attends a ball and there she meets the local aristocratic family the Osbornes, and Lord Osborne seems to take a liking to her. The novel ends around this point, with Austen leaving off writing after the sudden death of her father in 1805. It seems that Jane had planned to kill off Mr Watson and submit Emma to some stark financial circumstances, but facing the reality of this storyline herself, she abandoned the novel and never returned to it.

Austen's other unfinished work is the beginning of a novel called *Sanditon*. Jane began working on this novel soon after she finished *Persuasion* in 1817, calling it *The Brothers*. However, her rapidly deteriorating health meant she was forced to abandon the novel when she became too weak to even hold a pencil. The story was centered around a new spa town, Sanditon, and the fragment features some wonderfully comic characters, including the enterprising Mr Parker and his hypochondriac siblings. The novel is very different from Austen's other works, focusing again on the changing state of the world which she had commented on in *Persuasion*.

6

'What wild imaginations one forms where dear self is concerned! How sure to be mistaken!': Characters in Austen's novels

🐚 SENSE AND SENSIBILITY 🐚

Henry Dashwood

Father of Elinor, Marianne and Margaret, and father of John from his first marriage. He dies at the beginning of the novel.

Mrs Dashwood

Mother of Elinor, Marianne and Margaret and the second wife of Henry Dashwood. She cannot inherit her husband's estate and is forced to move when he dies. She refuses to check Marianne's extravagant behavior with Willoughby, and also fails to notice Elinor's hidden feelings for Edward. After Marianne's recovery from her near fatal illness Mrs Dashwood realizes the error of her ways and determines to live more sensibly.

John Dashwood

Son of Mr Dashwood, son-in-law of Mrs Dashwood, half brother of Marianne, Elinor and Margaret. John is responsible for the Dashwood women after his father's death but he gives them only a minimum income and spends the rest of the novel hoping they will marry wealthy men so that he doesn't have to support them.

Fanny Dashwood

Wife of John Dashwood, sister of Edward Ferrars. She is a proud and selfish woman who disapproves of the connection between Edward and Elinor and contrives to separate them. Although she claims to prefer Lucy Steele's company, when she learns of her secret engagement to Edward she throws her out into the street. Fanny is then forced to endure Lucy as her sister-in-law when Lucy marries Robert Ferrars.

Elinor Dashwood

Eldest daughter of Henry and Mrs Dashwood. She has feelings for Edward Ferrars but her sensible nature prevents her from expressing them. She tries to warn her younger sister Marianne against her unreserved emotions but in the end she must learn to display some of her own emotions. She marries Edward Ferrars and lives with him at his parsonage at Delaford.

Marianne Dashwood

Second daughter of Henry and Mrs Dashwood. Marianne is the epitome of 'sensibility', and is very open about her feelings for Willoughby, despite the associated scandal. She is then so devastated when he marries another woman that she becomes ill and almost dies. After this she resolves to live in a more sensible manner. She eventually marries Colonel Brandon.

Edward Ferrars

Fanny's brother and the son of Mrs Ferrars. He is described as not being a handsome man and, although kind, also has slightly awkward manners. He is secretly engaged to Lucy Steele for most of the novel, which leads to his disinheritance when the engagement is revealed. He enters the church but he is cast off by Lucy in favor of his younger brother Robert, who has now received Edward's inheritance. As soon as he is a free man he proposes to Elinor and takes up the living in the parish of Delaford.

Pocket Fact 👯

While Sense and Sensibility *(1995) was being filmed the Jane Austen society contacted the co-producer of the film to complain that Hugh Grant was too handsome to play Edward Ferrars.*

Margaret Dashwood

Youngest daughter of Henry and Mrs Dashwood. Margaret has one moment of significance in the novel, when she tells Elinor that she witnessed Willoughby taking a lock of Marianne's hair. At the end of the novel Margaret is old enough for dancing and becomes the point of focus for Sir John and Mrs Jennings', schemes.

John Willoughby

John Willoughby enters the novel as a dashing young gentleman who rescues Marianne after she falls. He and Marianne do not disguise their feelings for one another and so it is widely believed that they are engaged. However, he returns suddenly to London, ignores Marianne's letters and is cold and distant when they meet. He then writes revealing that he is actually engaged to another woman. At this point Colonel Brandon reveals Willoughby's true character, telling Elinor how Willoughby has seduced his ward and abandoned her when she became pregnant. Later Willoughby rushes to Somersetshire when he learns of Marianne's illness in order that he may explain his actions, saying he married Miss Grey purely for her fortune after his aunt cut him off for his behavior with Colonel Brandon's ward. He is then forced to live with the realization that if he had not acted in a selfish and extravagant way he could have married Marianne, the woman he loved, and had his inheritance.

Colonel Brandon

Colonel Brandon is an old friend of Sir John Middleton who owns the estate of Delaford. He is described as a quiet and serious man of 35. It is revealed that he suffered a terrible loss when the girl he loved was forced to marry his brother, and after a cruel marriage she died of consumption. He takes responsibility for her child, who is later seduced and abandoned by Willoughby. Once Marianne has matured beyond her romantic sensibilities she and the Colonel are married and prove an excellent match.

Eliza Williams

Eliza Williams is Colonel Brandon's ward and does not appear in the novel in person. Eliza's main role is to reveal Willoughby's true character when, after her disappearance, the Colonel finds she has been seduced and then abandoned by Willoughby when she became pregnant.

Mrs Jennings

Mrs Jennings is Sir John Middleton's mother-in-law, and the neighbor of the Dashwood women at Barton. She has two married daughters and so has turned her attention to marrying off the Dashwood girls. Although her jokes are sometimes embarrassing she is always well-meaning and helps Elinor to nurse Marianne while she is ill. At the end of the novel she has turned her focus on to finding a husband for Margaret.

Sir John Middleton

Sir John is Mrs Dashwood's cousin and offers the Dashwood women the living at Barton Cottage after their father's death. He is constantly arranging dances, outings and dinners at his home, and teases the Dashwood girls about their romantic interests. Like his mother-in-law, at the end of the novel he has turned his interests to Margaret and her future.

Lucy Steele

Lucy Steele is a cousin of Mrs Jennings, who, when staying at Barton, reveals to a shocked Elinor that she is secretly engaged to Edward Ferrars. Lucy is cruel and selfishly ambitious and manages to ingratiate herself with Fanny through her sycophancy. While staying with Fanny though Lucy's sister Anne reveals the truth of Lucy and Edward's engagement and an enraged Fanny throws Lucy out of her house. Edward stands by Lucy even though he is disinherited and they decide that he should enter the church. The next thing we hear of Lucy is when Edward reveals that she has married his brother Robert instead of him. Although Lucy and Robert Ferrars are dismissed by Mrs Ferrars after their shocking and sudden marriage, Lucy's skill for flattery eventually gains them an audience again.

Anne Steele

Lucy's sister. Most of her conversation revolves around her 'beaus', but she does provide Elinor with useful information about Lucy and Edward's relationship and is responsible for it becoming public.

Robert Ferrars

Edward's younger brother and a vain man. Robert inherits his mother's fortune when Edward is cast off, and unlike Edward, is given access to this inheritance immediately. He meets Lucy Steele to persuade her to break off her engagement to Edward but Lucy uses her skills of flattery to convince Robert to keep visiting her and eventually convinces him that she is now in love with him. They are married immediately and Robert prides himself on besting his brother.

❧ PRIDE AND PREJUDICE ❧

Mr Bennet

The long suffering husband of Mrs Bennet, and the father of Jane, Elizabeth, Mary, Kitty and Lydia. Mr Bennet spends most of his time in his library, preferring to laugh at the silly, and sometimes inappropriate, behavior of his wife and daughters instead of checking them. Elizabeth is his avowed favorite. He suffers a great blow when Lydia runs away with Wickham but he is saved from fulfilling his financial and paternal duties by Mr Darcy and his brother-in-law Mr Gardiner. Mr Bennet learns from his error with Lydia and after Elizabeth's marriage is a frequent visitor at Pemberley.

Mrs Bennet

The mother of the five Bennet girls and a consistently ridiculous woman. Her only purpose in life is to see her daughters married, and this goal, along with her 'nerves', make her a constant source of embarrassment to her two eldest daughters. Despite her wish to see Jane married to Bingley it is her own behavior in prompting this match that almost prevents it from happening.

By the end of the novel, although she has succeeded in having three daughters married, she is still said to be a very silly woman.

Jane Bennet

The eldest of the Bennet girls and acknowledged to be the prettiest. She has a kind and loving nature, sometimes even to her detriment as she refuses to believe ill of anyone. She meets Mr Bingley at the Meryton ball and likes him very much, but only reveals these feelings to Elizabeth, and suffers quietly when Darcy takes Bingley to London. Jane is Elizabeth's confidante throughout the novel and although she hides her feelings from everyone else by the end of the novel Bingley has been assured of Jane's regard for him and manages to find the courage to propose. They are a happy match and soon move to a house in Derbyshire near Pemberley.

Elizabeth Bennet

The heroine of the novel, and perhaps the feistiest of all Austen's heroines. She is never afraid to voice her opinion, as seen when she vehemently rejects Darcy's proposal and when she stands up to Lady Catherine. Throughout the novel Elizabeth gradually comes to realize how strong her feelings for Darcy are, but is sure he will not renew his advances towards her. The relationship between Darcy and Elizabeth is characterized by their witty exchanges and it is her vivacity and ability to speak her mind that makes Elizabeth such a well-liked character.

Pocket Fact 🕯

When Jane Austen was 20 she began work on her first draft of Pride and Prejudice, *making her the same age as her heroine Elizabeth Bennet. Austen would be 37 before the novel was published.*

Mary Bennet

Mary is the middle child in the Bennet family and is very serious and committed to her studies. She only contributes to conversations by offering some moral observation and is generally ignored by her family. By the end of the novel she is forced to socialize more after her sisters have left home and she benefits from not being compared to them constantly.

Kitty Bennet

Kitty (Catherine) Bennet is the second youngest Bennet girl, and she and her sister Lydia are very silly. They care only for balls and parties, and become obsessed with the militia and the officers while they are stationed there. Although she is devastated when she is not invited to Brighton along with Lydia, it actually saves her from ruining her reputation. Her father is strict with her after Lydia's poor behavior, and the good marriages made by Jane and Elizabeth introduce her to a better type of society which also improves her.

Lydia Bennet

The youngest of the Bennet girls, and the worst behaved. She cares only for parties and officers and acts as she pleases, not caring for her reputation or that of her family. She is allowed to go to Brighton and surpasses even Elizabeth's worst expectations when she elopes with Wickham. Once she is married she feels no sense of shame for her behavior, only boasting that she is first among her sisters to be married. Lydia and Wickham go to Newcastle, where they live in a constant state of debt.

Charles Bingley

The person who opens the novel, being the archetypal gentleman in possession of a good fortune, and therefore assumed to be in search of a wife. He takes possession of Netherfield Hall and from the beginning it is obvious that he loves Jane but his humble nature makes it easy for Darcy to convince him of Jane's indifference. By the end of the novel Darcy has told him the truth of Jane's affection and he eventually proposes.

Caroline Bingley

Bingley's unmarried sister, who unfortunately does not share his easy nature. She professes her regard for Jane, but clearly does not think her good enough for her brother, planning instead for him to marry Darcy's sister. Her jealous behavior towards Elizabeth arises from her acknowledgement of Darcy's admiration for her, and her behavior in trying to catch Darcy for herself may be seen as Austen's guide on how NOT to attract a husband. By the end of the novel she is still unmarried.

Fitzwilliam Darcy

Perhaps the most famous character from the novel, embodying the romantic ideal of countless women. He enters the novel as Bingley's friend and although the assembly at Meryton is interested in him after hearing of his vast fortune, his proud nature soon turns opinion against him. He fights against his feelings for Elizabeth, but after spending time with her at Netherfield he is decidedly in love with her. Later at Rosings he can no longer fight his feelings and proposes to Elizabeth, but in such a way as to deeply offend her. When he and Elizabeth suddenly meet again at Pemberley he is like a different man, both friendly and pleasant. He is there when Elizabeth receives the news about Lydia and Wickham, and as is revealed later, is the person to discover where they are hiding and arrange the marriage by paying off Wickham's debts. He comes to Longbourn and when Elizabeth thanks him for his help with Lydia, he confesses his feelings for her remain the same. They are engaged and are happily married. Despite his outward pride Darcy is a true gentleman and learns to be friendly and open through Elizabeth's influence.

Pocket Fact

Although Jane called her manuscript of Pride and Prejudice First Impressions *when she began writing it in 1796, by the time it was published in 1813 another novel had been published under this name, meaning she was forced to change the title.*

Georgiana Darcy

Darcy's younger sister, who is under his care after the death of their parents. Georgiana's main role in the novel is to reveal the true nature of Wickham when Darcy tells Elizabeth how Wickham seduced the 15 year old Georgiana out of revenge and in a bid to gain her fortune. Luckily Georgiana confessed about the elopement meaning Wickham fled, leaving her broken-hearted. Georgiana is thrilled when Darcy marries Elizabeth and learns from Elizabeth how to voice her opinion and stand up for herself.

Lady Catherine de Bourgh

Darcy's aunt, and Mr Collins' patroness. Lady Catherine symbolizes all the negative points of rank and birth, being extremely haughty and proud. She constantly interferes in other people's lives, offering advice on every topic from practising the piano to tending livestock. She arrives unexpectedly at Longbourn when she hears rumors of Elizabeth and Darcy's engagement and is furious when they marry, cutting them off for some time. She eventually recognizes the connection though and even condescends to visit Pemberley.

Charlotte Lucas

Elizabeth's friend and neighbor. Elizabeth is shocked when Charlotte uses flattery to secure Mr Collins, the very next day after Elizabeth has rejected his proposal. It is made clear that Charlotte is entering into this marriage as a source of financial security and to prevent herself from becoming an old maid. She represents what would have been a typical marriage, marrying a man from a sense of duty rather than because she truly loves him.

Mr Collins

Mr Collins is cousin to the Bennets and is set to inherit Longbourn. He arrives at Longbourn to seek reconciliation after a family rift, and quickly proves himself to be a ridiculous man. Lady Catherine has told him to find a wife and so he has come to Longbourn for that purpose. He proposes to Elizabeth and she has to reject him several times before he accepts it. While Mrs Bennet hopes he may look to one of her other daughters, Charlotte Lucas flatters him enough and he proposes to her instead.

Wickham

The handsome rogue. Wickham enters the militia when they are stationed in Meryton and soon becomes a favorite with everyone. He proceeds to tell Elizabeth how Darcy has cheated him out of the parsonage living promised to him by Darcy's father. Elizabeth is shocked and her dislike for Darcy increases. After receiving Darcy's letter, Elizabeth learns the truth about Wickham's past: that he refused the living and demanded money instead. When he later asked for more money and was refused, he set out to seduce Georgiana Darcy to gain access to her inheritance and get revenge on Darcy. Later, Lydia elopes with Wickham, and while he apparently had no intention of marrying Lydia, after receiving a bribe from Darcy, in the form of money and a commission in Newcastle, he agrees to the marriage. Wickham constantly lives beyond his means, even being so bold as to have Lydia write to Elizabeth asking Darcy for a living.

Mr and Mrs Gardiner

Mrs Bennet's brother and sister-in-law, and favorites with Jane and Elizabeth. After their tour in Derbyshire the Gardiners suspect that Darcy cares for Elizabeth, a suspicion further proved by his help with Lydia. The Gardiners are thrilled at the marriage of Darcy and Elizabeth and are frequent visitors at Pemberley, being credited by Elizabeth and Darcy as the people who brought them together.

❧ *MANSFIELD PARK* ❧

Fanny Price

The heroine of *Mansfield Park*, although she differs from Austen's other heroines in that she is shy, timid and afraid to speak. The novel is not so much about her romantic journey as about her observation of the romance occurring around her. Fanny is the daughter of Frances Bertram and Lieutenant Price, the niece of Mrs Norris, and Lady and Sir Thomas Bertram. Fanny arrives at Mansfield at the age of 10, after her mother writes to her estranged sisters asking for help, and she takes up a 'Cinderella' role in the house. Only her cousin Edmund shows her any kindness and she soon falls in love with him. During their residence at the nearby parsonage Fanny is forced to witness Mary and Henry Crawford's morally ambiguous influence, and watches Edmund fall in love with Mary. After witnessing Henry flirt with her two cousins, Fanny is disturbed when he proposes to her. Sir Thomas sends Fanny back to Portsmouth to live with her family in the hope that it will convince her to marry Henry, but a letter arrives revealing that Henry and the newly married Maria Bertram have run away together. Edmund comes to Portsmouth to take Fanny back to Mansfield, where Edmund slowly gets over Mary and soon comes to realize how much Fanny means to him. They marry and move into the parsonage at Mansfield Park.

Edmund Bertram

The younger son of Sir Thomas and Lady Bertram, and the only one of the family to show Fanny any kindness. It is intended that he will enter the church but his father is forced to let out the parsonage at Mansfield Park and Edmund has to put his career on hold. He is captivated by Mary Crawford when she comes to live at the parsonage and constantly blinds himself to her faults. Edmund is forced to see the true nature of Mary's character when she expresses her relaxed opinion on the affair between Maria and Henry. He slowly gets over her and in realizing her faults begins to see Fanny's strengths, soon realizing what a good match they are. They marry and Edmund becomes the curate at Mansfield Park.

Tom Bertram

The eldest son of Sir Thomas and Lady Bertram, Tom will inherit Mansfield Park. Tom is one of Austen's examples of a spoiled older son who has nothing to do but wait for his inheritance. He gambles so much that his father is forced to let out the parsonage intended for Edmund to pay his debts. Later in the novel Tom falls ill, and after he recovers, he is a changed man: more serious, with more care for the living he is set to inherit.

Maria Bertram

The eldest daughter of Sir Thomas and Lady Bertram. During her engagement to Mr Rushworth, Maria falls in love with Henry Crawford and flirts with him excessively. On her father's return Henry doesn't declare his feelings for Maria though and so she marries Mr Rushworth out of spite. Later, Henry and Maria run away together and she and Mr Rushworth are divorced. When Henry refuses to marry her, she is forced to move in with her aunt Norris as no decent society will accept her.

Julia Bertram

The younger daughter of the Bertram family. Julia also flirts with Henry but during the play she realizes his preference for her sister and gives up Henry entirely. When Maria is married to Mr Rushworth Julia accompanies her sister to London, where, after Maria's affair, Julia elopes with Mr Yates so that she can avoid being blamed for Maria's actions.

Lady Bertram

The wife of Sir Thomas, aunt to Fanny, sister to Mrs Norris and Mrs Price, and mother to Tom, Maria, Julia and Edmund. Lady Bertram is presented as a lazy, stupid woman who cares more for her dog than her children. She is often clueless about the real state of affairs, including the moral ambiguity of the play scheme and the severity of Tom's illness. She realizes how much Fanny means to her while she is in Portsmouth, and is happy when Susan, Fanny's younger sister comes to Mansfield to take Fanny's place when Fanny marries Edmund.

Sir Thomas Bertram

The father of Tom, Edmund, Maria and Julia, and uncle to Fanny. He resolves to adopt Fanny when she is a child but is keen to maintain the social differences between her and his children. Sir Thomas doesn't become as involved in his children's lives as he should, but on his return from Antigua he is pleased at the improvement in Fanny's looks and begins to treat her more kindly. He has some doubts about Maria's wedding but allows her to marry Mr Rushworth anyway, a mistake he later comes to regret. After both his daughters elope Sir Thomas is forced to realize the mistakes he has made, and is pleased when Fanny and Edmund decide to marry.

Mrs Norris

The elder sister of Lady Bertram and Mrs Price. Mrs Norris is the main instigator for the cruel treatment of Fanny, constantly reminding her of her lower social standing and using her as a servant. Mrs Norris spoils Maria and Julia and gives herself credit for the match with Mr Rushworth. She is bitterly disappointed by Maria's affair with Henry. Sir Thomas grows increasingly weary of Mrs Norris and her frugal ways, and after Maria leaves Henry he sends Mrs Norris to live with her.

Mary Crawford

The sister of Mrs Grant and Henry. On first arriving at Mansfield she intends to make Tom Bertram fall in love with her, but she is dismayed to find she has growing feelings for Edmund, the younger son. She eventually decides that she will be able to convince Edmund to marry her and give her the lifestyle she desires, so befriends Fanny to ingratiate herself with Edmund. Mary's downfall comes about when discussing the affair between Henry and Maria: she is not shocked at their actions, only that they didn't take enough care not to get caught. Edmund is outraged at these sentiments and after they argue he leaves and never sees Mary again. The last thing we hear of Mary is that she has gone to live with Mrs Grant after Dr Grant's death.

Henry Crawford

The brother of both Mary and Mrs Grant. Henry's behavior is shocking as he pays his attentions to Maria rather than Julia, claiming that engaged women are always more attractive. Later Henry is stunned at how much Fanny dislikes him and decides to make Fanny fall in love with him, although he actually falls in love with her himself and proposes to her. Despite her refusal he is determined not to give her up, even coming to see her at Portsmouth. Henry's character improves and he is making progress with Fanny when he meets Maria again in London and she leaves her husband for him. The novel ends with Henry suffering under the knowledge that if he had not given in to his vanity to win Maria he would have eventually won Fanny.

Mrs Price

The middle sister of the Ward sisters and mother to Fanny and William. She makes an imprudent match, marrying a sailor below her class and becomes estranged from her family. After having several children and struggling for money she writes to her sisters to ask for help, and sends Fanny to live with them. When Fanny returns to Portsmouth she finds her mother is not affectionate, but is lazy and selfish. She is not caring towards Fanny during her stay there and after her departure we hear nothing more of her.

William Price

Fanny's older brother, and the only member of her family that she keeps in touch with. Sir Thomas helps him in his naval career and William writes to Fanny during his periods at sea. On one of his shore leaves he comes to visit her at Mansfield, bringing her a cross which Fanny wears at the ball Sir Thomas organizes. Henry Crawford uses his family connections in the navy to make William a second lieutenant.

Mrs Grant

The older half sister of Henry and Mary Crawford. She is married to Dr Grant, who becomes the parson at Mansfield Park. She is keen to find spouses for Mary and Henry and encourages their relationship with the Bertram family. After the death of Dr Grant she moves in with Mary Crawford.

Dr Grant

Dr Grant becomes the parson at Mansfield when Sir Thomas is forced to let out the living. He is a poor example of a clergyman, and dies at the end of the novel after having three decadent dinners in one week.

Mr Rushworth

The owner of Sotherton, an estate worth £12,000 a year (about $612,000 now). He becomes engaged to Maria Bertram and is mortified by Maria's behavior with Henry during the play. When Sir Thomas returns from Antigua the couple are married and go to London. We hear no more of Mr Rushworth until it is revealed that Maria has run away with Henry Crawford, forcing him to divorce her.

Mr Yates

A slight acquaintance of Tom Bertram's who comes to stay at Mansfield. He is the person to inspire the theaterical scheme at Mansfield and the most enthusiastic actor of the group. He suffers bad luck when Sir Thomas returns and cancels the play. We next hear of Mr Yates when the news reaches Mansfield that Julia has eloped with him.

Susan Price

Fanny's younger sister, whom Fanny grows close to on her return to Portsmouth. Susan has the most refined manners in the Price family but she is still rough and uneducated. Fanny undertakes to educate her, and guides her in her reading and conduct. Susan goes back to Mansfield with Fanny and takes Fanny's place as companion to Lady Bertram when Fanny marries Edmund.

🐚 EMMA 🐚

Emma Woodhouse

The titular character, the only one of Austen's heroines to be so. Throughout the novel we see that Emma is too admired by everyone around her, and she is allowed to be mistress of her own home following the death of her mother and the marriage of her elder sister. The only person who criticizes Emma is her neighbor and brother-in-law Mr Knightley, who tries to guide her judgment and behavior. After making several errors in judgment by the end of the novel Emma has realized she is in love with Mr Knightley, and has resolved to behave according to the high standard he sets for her. Despite her flaws and blatant misjudgments Emma is one of Austen's most beloved heroines.

Mr Woodhouse

Emma's elderly father. He is very specific about how he lives his life, and hates change of any kind. Mr Woodhouse constantly consults his doctor Mr Perry and is afraid of every circumstance from riding in a carriage to having windows open in the summer. Mr Woodhouse is one of Austen's most comical characters and even though Emma has a lot to put up with caring for her father, you cannot help but laugh when Mr Woodhouse recommends thin gruel over wedding cake.

Mr (George) Knightley

The owner of the neighboring estate to Hartfield, and a daily visitor at the Woodhouse home. He chastises Emma for her poor behavior and consistently acts well himself, such as when he asks Harriet to dance at the ball. He dislikes Frank Churchill and it becomes clear at the end of the novel that this arises from jealousy as he has been in love with Emma for years. In choosing to marry Emma, Mr Knightley knows he must now put up with Mr Woodhouse and graciously offers to move to Hartfield so that he and Emma may marry without leaving her father alone.

Harriet Smith

A pupil at Mrs Goddard's school in Highbury village, who is thought by everyone to be very pretty, albeit of a lower social class. Emma takes a liking to Harriet though and decides to improve her. Her worst influence on Harriet comes when she persuades her to refuse a marriage offer from Robert Martin, a local farmer. Harriet thinks herself in love with both Mr Elton and Mr Knightley during the novel and is disappointed when they both marry other women, Emma herself being one of them. Harriet then realizes she has always loved Robert Martin and finally accepts his proposal. She and Robert marry and her friendship with Emma gradually fades as befits their different social standings.

Mrs Weston (Miss Taylor)

Mrs Weston begins the novel as Miss Taylor, Emma's former governess who marries Mr Weston and moves to the nearby estate of Randalls. Mrs Weston does try to moderate Emma's behavior but she isn't as successful as Mr Knightley as she loves her too much. Mrs Weston remains close to Emma throughout the novel and even tries to set her up with her son-in-law Frank Churchill.

Mr Weston

The owner of Randalls estate, who marries Emma's former governess Miss Taylor. Mr Weston is a cheerful and easy-going man who loves company. Mr Weston has a son from his first marriage, Frank Churchill, whom he is keen to include in Highbury society.

Frank Churchill

Mr Weston's son from his first marriage. He is a sociable, handsome young man set to inherit a large fortune from his demanding aunt, who adopted him as a child. Frank Churchill comes to Highbury and flirts with Emma constantly and while Emma initially thinks she loves him she soon realizes she only cares for him as a friend. After Frank's aunt dies he returns suddenly to Highbury and announces the shocking news that he has been secretly engaged to Jane Fairfax for months. After Frank apologizes for his deceptive behavior, the local society are pleased at the match, and it is hoped that Jane's superior nature will improve Frank.

Jane Fairfax

The niece of Miss Bates and the granddaughter of Mrs Bates. Jane is an orphan who was adopted and raised alongside Colonel Campbell's daughter. After Miss Campbell's marriage Jane comes to stay with Miss and Mrs Bates. Jane's health suffers as a result of the stress of hiding her engagement to Frank and eventually she decides to break it off. As a poor orphan her only option then is to accept a post as a governess, but Frank comes to Highbury and convinces her to take him back. Jane becomes much less reserved and she and Emma become friends.

Mr Elton

The local clergyman. Emma decides that he will be a good match for Harriet and after her intensive match-making is very shocked when Mr Elton proposes to her instead. In listening to her refusal Mr Elton reveals that he thinks very highly of himself and means to marry well. He proves this by going to Bath and marrying a young lady who is wealthy but not from a respectable family. His punishment is then to be left with a wife who tries to control everyone.

Mrs Elton

Mr Elton's bride, and Austen's depiction of new money that has forgotten its roots. Mrs Elton constantly boasts of her brother-in-law's wealth and tries to establish herself as the first woman in Highbury society. On receiving a less than warm reception from Emma, Mrs Elton turns her attention instead to Jane Fairfax and constantly tries to get her a place as a governess. At the end of the novel Mrs Elton is one of the only people not to approve of the match between Mr Knightley and Emma.

Miss Bates

The poor spinster of Highbury and Jane's aunt. She had been part of a wealthy family but a loss in fortune has left her and her elderly mother in a small house struggling to make ends meet. Miss Bates is the most talkative character in all of Austen's novels and it is difficult for others to get a word in edgewise.

Isabella Knightley

Emma's sister, and wife of Mr Knightley's brother. She lives in London with her husband and children, and like her father constantly worries over the health of her family.

John Knightley

Mr Knightley's younger brother and Emma's brother-in-law. Emma often finds him too impatient with her father and he can be grumpy and ill-tempered. He does mean well though, and proves to be as astute as his brother when he guesses that Mr Elton has designs on Emma.

Robert Martin

A farmer on Mr Knightley's estate. He proposes to Harriet Smith at the beginning of the novel but is refused. Emma meets him and is surprised to find him so well-spoken and polite but she is still very aware of the difference in their social positions. Despite Harriet's refusal Robert continues to love her and by the end of the novel he is rewarded when she accepts his renewed proposal.

❦ NORTHANGER ABBEY ❦

Catherine Morland

The heroine of the novel. At the age of 17 she is invited to go to Bath with her neighbors where she will experience balls and refined society. Catherine meets Henry Tilney, a handsome young man whom she instantly falls in love with. Catherine's blatant portrayal of her feelings for Henry, and her caring and humble personality, make him treat her kindly and tease her when she allows her imagination to be too influenced by Gothic novels. Catherine is victim to a plot twist when General Tilney is misled about her fortune, causing him to first court her affection for his son, and then to throw her out the house when he learns she is not as rich as he supposes. This event causes Henry to defend Catherine, and come to her home in Fullerton to propose to her.

Henry Tilney

A handsome young clergyman who asks to be introduced to Catherine at a ball in Bath. He is a polite young man, who despite his regular teasing of Catherine is very kind to her, and treats her well. He is also kind to his sister Eleanor, often returning home to Northanger Abbey from his own home at Woodston to ensure she is not lonely. Henry is witty and clever and tries to teach Catherine to think beyond her own naive ideas, eventually returning her affections.

Eleanor Tilney

Henry's sister, who becomes Catherine's friend. Eleanor must endure a harsh life at Northanger, constantly having to follow her father's orders. Eleanor is kind and caring like her brother, and the novel ends happily when she marries a Viscount whom she has cared for for a long time.

Isabella Thorpe

Catherine's first friend in Bath. Isabella is a vivacious flirt, with no fortune of her own, and hoping to marry well. She first sets her sights on James Morland, Catherine's brother, but as soon as she secures him she becomes interested in Captain Tilney. James eventually tires of this treatment and breaks off the engagement. At this point the Captain ceases his attentions and soon leaves Bath, leaving Isabella with nothing. She writes to Catherine asking for her assistance to win back James but Catherine has now become aware of her real character and does not even answer her letter.

John Thorpe

Isabella's brash, rude and arrogant brother who cares mostly about his horse and carriage. He sets his sights on Catherine and in his boasting of his wealth and possessions, makes himself very disagreeable. It is John who misleads the General about Catherine's wealth, first exaggerating when he hopes to marry her, and then describing her as practically destitute when he learns that she has not accepted his advances.

Mr Allen

Catherine's neighbor who takes her to Bath. He often leaves Mrs Allen and Catherine to go play cards, and only acts as her chaperone when he tells her she shouldn't go out in the carriage with John Thorpe.

Mrs Allen

Mr Allen's wife: a superficial woman who cares only for her appearance. She is not a very good chaperone, always more occupied by the fashion around her than what is happening to Catherine.

Captain Frederick Tilney

Henry and Eleanor's elder brother. He arrives in Bath after James and Isabella are engaged and immediately begins flirting with Isabella. The Captain continues to pay his attentions to Isabella, until James breaks off their engagement, at which point he leaves Bath, indicating that his attentions were never serious.

James Morland

Catherine's elder brother, who becomes engaged to Isabella while in Bath. He cares for her deeply and after enduring her flirting with Captain Tilney, breaks off their engagement and returns to Oxford.

General Tilney

The owner of Northanger Abbey, and father of Frederick, Henry and Eleanor. He is a strict man who demands that everything be done according to his wishes and timetable. He is a greedy man who is only kind to Catherine because he believes she will receive a large inheritance. When he learns this isn't true he unceremoniously throws her out of his house. He forbids Henry from seeing Catherine but Henry defies him and proposes to her. It is only Eleanor's marriage to the wealthy Viscount that softens the General enough to consent to Catherine and Henry's marriage.

Mrs Morland

Catherine's mother. Mrs Morland is a great advocate for common sense, but doesn't realize that Catherine is in love when she returns from Northanger Abbey, instead chastizing her for allowing her head to be turned by the grandeur of her adventures. When she meets Henry Mrs Morland likes him and is pleased by his proposal to her daughter.

☙ PERSUASION ☙

Anne Elliot

The central character in the novel. When Anne was only 19 she had formed an engagement with Captain Wentworth but was persuaded to break it off by her godmother. About seven years later Anne is suddenly thrown into close company with Captain Wentworth again when his sister rents Kellynch Hall from her father, and while he is cold at first he warms up and Anne begins to hope he may still care for her. After a conversation in which Anne defends women as loving the longest, Captain Wentworth writes confessing that he still loves her. Anne immediately finds him and the engagement they had broken off is reformed. She is loyal to her friends, choosing to visit her poor invalid friend Mrs Smith rather than waiting on her wealthy cousin Lady Dalrymple. Anne is often overlooked by her own family but is a great favorite with the Musgroves and the Crofts for her sensible and intelligent nature.

Captain Frederick Wentworth

The main romantic interest in the novel Captain Wentworth is 'brilliant' and 'full of life and ardor'. Lady Russell is put off by Captain Wentworth's lack of rank as well as his headstrong confidence and so persuades Anne to break off their engagement. When he returns from abroad he is cold towards Anne and soon forms a preference for Louisa. On a visit to Lyme though the Captain misses Louisa when she jumps from some steps and she falls and injures her head. When she begins to recover he realizes he doesn't really care for her, and fears he has trapped himself. Luckily he is freed from any obligation when Louisa becomes engaged to Captain Benwick. Captain Wentworth immediately rushes to Bath to be near Anne and jealously watches her relationship with Mr Elliot, but on hearing Anne profess women's capability to love for years with no hope he takes the courage to write to her and tell her he loves her. Captain Wentworth is a kind and noble man, caring deeply for his fellow naval officers and his family.

Sir Walter Elliot

Anne's father and the owner of Kellynch Hall. Sir Walter is a proud, vain man who cares only for rank and beauty. Since the death of his wife he has had no check on his extravagant spending habits, meaning he is forced to rent out his inherited estate to pay off his debts. Although there is some fear that Sir Walter will fall prey to Mrs Clay's scheme to marry him, he is saved by Mr Elliot's desperation to inherit his title. At the end of the novel Sir Walter gives his permission for Anne to marry Captain Wentworth.

Elizabeth Elliot

Anne's elder sister, and her father's favorite. Elizabeth is the lady of Kellynch Hall but at the age of 29 she longs to be married.

Elizabeth is cruel to Anne, preferring the companionship of her friend Mrs Clay to her sister's. Although Elizabeth imagines Mr Elliot is in love with her, she must face the humiliation of his leaving when Anne becomes engaged.

Lady Russell

Anne's godmother and the late Lady Elliot's friend. She lives near Kellynch and takes special care of Anne, even persuading her to break off the engagement to Captain Wentworth as she believed it was best for Anne. Later in the novel Lady Russell tries to persuade Anne to accept Mr Elliot's advances, tempting her with the idea of becoming Lady Elliot. When the truth of Mr Elliot's character emerges, and Anne accepts Captain Wentworth, Lady Russell is forced to reconsider her opinions.

Mary Musgrove (née Elliot)

Sir Walter's youngest daughter. Her only achievement has been to marry a nearby landowner, Charles Musgrove. Mary is not as cruel to Anne as Elizabeth but she is very selfish, and suffers from the Elliot pride as much as her father and sister. Mary is silly and selfish and often fancies herself unwell. She is pleased at Anne's marriage but mainly because Anne does not outrank her.

Charles Musgrove

Mary's husband, and Louisa and Henrietta's brother. Charles suffers from Mary's constant nagging and could have become a better man if he had chosen a better wife. He is a kind and simple man who prefers hunting and shooting to anything else.

Mr and Mrs Musgrove

Parents to Charles, Louisa and Henrietta. They are very fond of Anne and greatly appreciate her help after Louisa's accident. They are loving parents to their large family, often hosting parties and making no objections to either Louisa or Henrietta's marriages.

Louisa Musgrove

Mary's sister-in-law and one of the eldest Musgrove daughters. Louisa becomes besotted with Captain Wentworth and when she expresses her conviction that a person must be firm in her decisions and not be easily persuaded it seems that she has won him. However this same free spiritedness leads Louisa to ignore Captain Wentworth, meaning she falls from some stone stairs, and suffers a head injury. After a long illness she suffers from terrible nerves and becomes a much quieter person. During her recovery Louisa unexpectedly falls in love with Captain Benwick and they are soon engaged.

Henrietta Musgrove

The other Musgrove daughter. She, like Louisa, is also infatuated with Captain Wentworth and even admires him so much that she damages her relationship with her cousin Charles Hayter. Although Henrietta seems undecided which man she truly loves, she is persuaded by her sister to visit Charles Hayter, and their relationship is soon rekindled. They enter into an engagement and although Charles Hayter does not have a large fortune, Henrietta's parents allow her to marry rather than suffering through a long engagement.

Charles Hayter

The Musgrove's cousin, a clergyman who is set to inherit the nearby estate of Winthrop. He is very disturbed when he sees Henrietta's growing attachment to Captain Wentworth, but after Henrietta's visit their relationship is soon rekindled. They are engaged and Charles Hayter convinces the Musgroves to allow them to marry straight away.

Captain Benwick

A friend of Captain Wentworth's from the navy. Captain Benwick had been engaged to Captain Harville's sister but they postponed their marriage while he went into the navy to make his fortune. Sadly Fanny Harville died before he could return and when Anne meets him he is a quiet, withdrawn man who constantly reads poetry. During Louisa's illness Benwick spends a lot of time with her and in teaching her about poetry, manages to get over Fanny and fall in love with Louisa.

Captain Harville

Another of Captain Wentworth's naval friends. Captain Harville is a kind man, who despite his war injury is very industrious around the house. Captain Harville and his wife kindly give up a room in their house to Louisa during her recovery, and Mrs Harville nurses her diligently.

Mr William Elliot

The Elliots' cousin. In his youth Mr Elliot despised his cousins and had no respect for the title he was to inherit from Sir Walter. He refused all invitations to visit Kellynch and purchased his independence from his family by marrying a wealthy woman of low connections, who later dies leaving her entire fortune to Mr Elliot. When Anne arrives in Bath she finds that Mr Elliot has reconciled with her family and is now a regular visitor at the house. Anne is charmed by his manners but does feel that he is not totally open, and soon learns that he is a cruel man who treated her friend Mrs Smith very poorly. It turns out that he is paying his attentions to Anne to ensure that he inherits the title, even offering to keep Mrs Clay as his mistress to ensure she doesn't marry Sir Walter. He eventually moves back to London, taking Mrs Clay with him to ensure he doesn't miss out on the inheritance which now means so much to him.

Admiral Croft

Captain Wentworth's brother-in-law. He is a charming, open man whom Anne gets along with very well. The Admiral and Mrs Croft comprise the best example of a marriage in Austen's novels, being equal partners who bring out the best in one another.

Mrs Sophia Croft

Captain Wentworth's sister. Mrs Croft is an impressive figure, having been at sea with her husband several times, traveling the world and living on board the ship in cramped conditions. She chastises Captain Wentworth for saying women cannot live on ship, arguing instead that women are sensible, rational creatures – Austen's most blatant inclusion of the feminist attitudes emerging in her day.

Mrs Clay

The daughter of Sir Walter's lawyer. She becomes Elizabeth's friend and is invited to accompany her to Bath. Both Anne and Lady Russell worry that Mrs Clay is trying to catch him as a husband. Mr Elliot also worries about this, so much so that he offers to set Mrs Clay up as his mistress in order to prevent her from marrying Sir Walter.

Mrs Smith

An old school friend of Anne's who has fallen on hard times. It is Mrs Smith who reveals the truth of Mr Elliot's character, telling Anne how he forced her husband into debt and then refused to help her financially. Mrs Smith suffers from a rheumatic fever and is forced to live life as an invalid. When Anne marries Captain Wentworth, he helps Mrs Smith to recover her lost fortune.

Dowager Viscountess Dalrymple

A high-ranking cousin of the Elliots. The only role Lady Dalrymple plays in the novel is to highlight the extent to which Elizabeth and Sir Walter value rank and title, and at the end of the novel, their sycophantic flattery of their titled cousin is all they have left.

7

'A lady's imagination is very rapid; it jumps from admiration to love, from love to matrimony in a moment':
Love, romance and marriage in Austen's novels

For many readers the most enjoyable parts of Austen's novels are the romantic adventures of her heroines and memorable leading men. The dynamics of these timeless relationships can be confusing though: why is it such a scandal that Jane Fairfax and Frank Churchill are secretly engaged, and why is it so shocking that Elizabeth Bennet and Anne Elliot turn down marriage proposals? This chapter will guide you through the intricate courtship rituals of Regency relationships, as well as looking at Jane Austen's own romantic encounters.

🐚 JANE AUSTEN'S OWN LOVE LIFE 🐚

Many of Jane Austen's readers are surprised when they discover that the author who created such delightful romances was herself never married. While it is true that Jane never married, she did have some memorable romantic encounters.

THE MYSTERIOUS CLERGYMAN

It is known that in 1802 Jane and her family were traveling through Devon and the coast. While on this trip, it is suspected that Jane had a brief romantic encounter which wouldn't seem out of place in one of her novels. After Jane's death, her sister Cassandra recalled that Jane had met a young man who was very taken with the authoress and wanted to meet her again.

Unfortunately the news soon reached them that this young man had unexpectedly died. It has been suggested that this young man was Samuel Blackall, a clergyman whom Jane had met in Steventon in 1797. While it is not known how attached Jane was to this young man (or even if he was Samuel Blackall) both Dorset and Lyme Regis feature as romantic meeting places in her novels (in *Emma* and *Persuasion* respectively) and it is poignant that Lyme Regis in *Persuasion* is the scene of a love thwarted by the untimely death of one of the lovers.

TOM LEFROY

The earliest surviving letter we have of Jane Austen's is one written to Cassandra in the winter of 1795. In the letter, Jane makes mention of a Tom Lefroy, the nephew of Jane's good friend Mrs Lefroy. Jane's letter teases her sister by describing how she and 'her Irish friend', both aged 20 at the time, behaved shockingly, telling Cassandra to imagine, 'everything most profligate and shocking in the way of dancing and sitting down together'. Jane's letter shows her happiness in this blossoming romance with a handsome, clever young Irish man. Her letter tells Cassandra that Tom called on her the day after the ball and although she says she does not like his coat, she does mention that they have discussed *Tom Jones* by Fielding, a scandalous conversation for her to be having with a young man since the book openly discusses sexual acts and illegitimate children. At this point in her life it is likely that Jane would have imagined herself settling down with Tom. However her next letter has a change of tone, telling Cassandra that, 'The day is come on which I am to flirt my last with Tom Lefroy, & when you receive this it will be over'. Jane mocks herself by talking of 'the tears which flow as I write' but it is clear to see that she was disappointed at his departure.

It seems that although Jane and Tom probably were in love, the romance wasn't meant to be. Tom was the eldest son of a large family whom he had to support back in Ireland. He was studying law in London with the support of a wealthy uncle and the expectations of his family meant that he couldn't marry a poor clergyman's daughter. In 1796 Tom's aunt sent him back to London and it is likely that Jane never saw him again. In 1798 Tom returned to Ireland and in 1799 he married a wealthy heiress, Mary Paul. Tom had a successful career and would eventually go on to become the Lord Chief Justice of Ireland. Although Jane never saw Tom again, her niece Anna later married Tom's nephew Ben.

Jane meanwhile now knew what it meant to love and lose, and this experience gives a sense of reality to the pain felt by all of her heroines at one point or another in their own romantic entanglements. Jane now turned to her writing, and devoted herself to it completely. In October 1796 (just after Tom's departure) she began work on *First Impressions* and after completing it in November 1797 she began reworking *Elinor and Marianne*.

Pocket Fact 🔱

It seems that Jane's thwarted love affair with Tom Lefroy not only inspired her own work but a host of other stories as well. The film Becoming Jane, *starring Anne Hathaway and James McAvoy, focuses on this relationship, and in 1997 the BBC broadcast a radio play called* Jane and Tom: The Real Pride and Prejudice.

HARRIS BIGG-WITHER

In 1802 Jane Austen received her only offer of marriage, from Harris Bigg-Wither, the brother of her good friends, Mary, Catherine and Althea. Harris was five years younger than Jane and was probably encouraged by his sisters to propose to Jane. Jane was now 27 and it was an attractive prospect for her to marry a wealthy landowner, with an estate only five miles from her old home at Steventon. By marrying Harris, Jane would be able to support her sister Cassandra and enjoy the security of being a wealthy wife. Jane accepted Harris and there was much celebration. However, overnight Jane had a change of heart and the next day told Harris that she could not accept his proposal. Jane's niece Catherine later described Jane's acceptance as, 'A momentary fit of self delusion'. Soon after this rejection Harris went on to marry a girl from the Isle of Wight, while Jane, with her last chance of marriage gone, devoted herself to her writing, revising *Northanger Abbey*, and making her work the true love of her life.

Other reasons Jane Austen didn't marry

Aside from not being able to be with the man she wanted to spend her life with, there are a few other factors which may have contributed to Jane's decision not to marry:

- In 1797 Cassandra's fiancé Tom Fowle died at sea. Tom had been serving as a chaplain in the navy but died of yellow fever before he could return. Cassandra never met anyone else, choosing at the age of just 24 to become a spinster. Jane's own thwarted love affair, combined with her sister's disappointment, may have contributed to her decision to remain single.

- By not marrying Jane was also free from the expectation that she would run a household, giving her the freedom and leisure to write. Jane learned to value the freedom of being single as she watched those around her become slave to the expected roles of wife and mother.

Pocket Fact ♔

Although Jane never had children of her own, she often referred to her novels as her children, saying, 'I am never too busy to think of S&S. I can no more forget it, than a mother can forget her suckling child'. At another time she referred to Pride and Prejudice *as, 'my own darling child'.*

⚜ MARRYING IN JANE ⚜ AUSTEN'S TIME

In choosing not to marry, Jane became a spinster, choosing her love of her writing over the expectations of society. But for those who did marry what did marriage mean? And how did one go about finding a partner?

COURTSHIP

When looking for a partner in Regency society, it was vital that a potential partner was eligible – meaning they were from the right class of society and were wealthy enough to meet family expectations. Young men had to ensure that the lady they were addressing was 'out', meaning that the girl was over 16 (the age a girl could marry at) and had formally come out into society. Young men on the other hand would 'come out' at 21, meaning most husbands were older than their wives (as is the case for most of the matches in Austen's novels). This was because for the eldest sons who were set to inherit, this was the age that they no longer needed their father's consent to enter into a contract, including an engagement. For gentlemen who didn't have an inheritance coming, the older age meant that they had time to establish their career and raise enough money to support a wife and family.

During Austen's lifetime young men and women would normally meet at dances, or would be introduced through family and friends. When young people did meet, a young lady would always be accompanied by a chaperone, meaning couples had very little chance for one-on-one conversation. Dancing provided a chance for some private conversation, but it was only acceptable for a couple to dance together twice before it was considered that an arrangement existed between them. Apart from dancing, young people could also meet at family parties, where they could play cards, join in conversation with the rest of the family, or perhaps even perform a duet together. It is obvious therefore that couples did not get the chance to spend any time alone together. In fact it was very much frowned upon for young men and women to be alone together, either walking or riding together. We see the scandal it causes when Marianne constantly goes out in Willoughby's gig (a type of carriage, see glossary), and Catherine's worry about going out with John Thorpe. A couple couldn't even write to each other until they were engaged, once again showing why Elinor is convinced Marianne is engaged to Willoughby when she sees Marianne sending him several letters. In never being alone together it seems that Charlotte Lucas may have been right: 'Happiness in marriage is entirely a matter of chance'.

In Her Own Words 🖤

Jane once sarcastically wrote to her niece Fanny that, 'Single Women have a dreadful propensity for being poor — which is one very strong argument in favor of Matrimony'.

The role of mothers in matchmaking

Austen's novels are all courtship novels, meaning that nearly all of the action within them revolves around finding and winning a partner. What Austen's novels also show is how much mothers would be involved in making this match.

Top matchmaking/meddling mothers

1. **Mrs Bennet (*Pride and Prejudice*)**. *The ultimate meddling mother, whose only purpose in life is to find husbands for her daughters. Mrs Bennet spends almost the entirety of the novel making matches for her daughters. Although she frequently embarrasses her daughters, she is the most successful matchmaker in Austen's novels with three of her five daughters married by the end of the novel.*
2. **Lady Russell (*Persuasion*)**. *Makes a terrible job of trying to see Anne happily married. She dissuades her from marrying the man she really loves and spends a large part of the novel trying to persuade her to marry a man who turns out to be a complete scoundrel.*
3. **Mrs Weston (*Emma*)**. *Emma's former governess, who tries to match Emma with her new son-in-law, Frank Churchill. Emma doesn't really care for Frank though and is distracted by her own matchmaking schemes. This is*

lucky because Frank is secretly engaged to another woman for the entire novel!

4. **Mrs Thorpe (Northanger Abbey)**. Probably the most realistic representation of a matchmaking Regency mother. Mrs Thorpe is a widow with only a small income who pushes her daughter to find a rich husband, as we see when she openly discusses the settlement from Mr Morland. Mrs Thorpe turns out to be rather unsuccessful though as her mercenary encouragements cause Isabella to drive both interested men away.

5. **Mrs Dashwood (Sense and Sensibility)**. Allows her daughter Marianne too much freedom in her relationship with Willoughby, while at the same time not realizing how much Elinor cares for Edward.

6. **Sir Thomas Bertram (Mansfield Park)**. OK he's a man but as his wife is too lazy, Sir Thomas is forced to act as a matchmaker instead. He proves to be terrible though, allowing Maria to marry a man she despises for money, meaning she later has an affair and leaves her husband. Sir Thomas' other daughter Julia also elopes. Sir Thomas also tries to force Fanny to marry a man she clearly dislikes and sends her away from the house when she refuses to do so.

PROPOSALS

Once a young man had seen enough (or as much as was acceptable!) of a young woman to decide that he wanted to marry her how did he ask her to be his wife? The proposal was often the first time a young couple would be alone together and he would ask the lady to accept him. This would normally take place at her family home and while engagement rings did exist, they weren't common. At this point the young lady could accept or refuse the proposal. As Henry Tilney points out this 'power of refusal' was the only control women held in the situation. It was rare for a young woman to refuse a proposal though since, as Mr Collins points out to Elizabeth, if a lady had been proposed to once already she was unlikely to receive another proposal. The only other power a woman possessed was the ability to pull out of an engagement. Again, this was a very rare occurrence (although Jane Austen herself did this!). Once an engagement had been formed it was highly frowned upon for a man to break it off, hence Edward's feeling of being trapped in his engagement to Lucy.

If a young man was accepted, he would then go to the young lady's father to ask permission to marry his daughter. Sometimes he would also ask his own father, as James Morland does in *Northanger Abbey*. Once a young lady's father had approved the match (which he would normally have witnessed developing from the beginning), the marriage articles would be drawn up. This was a contract outlining the distribution of wealth and property in the marriage and what would happen to the wife and any children on the death of the husband (marriage articles were a bit like pre-nuptial agreements drawn up today.) A jointure might also be drawn up – an agreement outlining that the wife would be guaranteed to receive part of her husband's property on his death – although these were more unusual.

Pocket Fact 🕯

At the 2009 Jane Austen Festival in Bath, one couple decided to honor their favorite author by having a Regency style wedding. The ceremony took place one afternoon during the festival and all of the guests were required to wear Regency dress. It does make one wonder if there was enough lace to satisfy Mrs Elton though!

WEDDINGS

Before the wedding a bride would go shopping for her wedding clothes, purchasing the entire wardrobe of clothes she would now need as a wife and mistress of her own home. The actual wedding dress wasn't as important as it is now – normally a bride would wear her best dress, which was usually a white dress as white was a sign of wealth. The groom in the meantime would be busy preparing his home for the bride's arrival and traditionally buying a new coach.

The wedding ceremony would take place in the morning and the party would then go for a wedding breakfast. Immediately after the breakfast the couple would set off on their honeymoon, while their guests enjoyed the wedding cake (apart from Mr Woodhouse who would worry it is too rich!).

Pocket Fact ⚜

Considering that most of the action in her novels leads up to a proposal from the leading man, surprisingly, most of the proposals that occur in Jane's novels aren't laid out word for word. Austen, as the narrator, normally just describes that the moment has occurred. Only in Pride and Prejudice *and* Persuasion *are we witness to the word-for-word confessions of love from the leading man: in Darcy's second confession of love to Elizabeth, and in Captain Wentworth's letter to Anne.*

ELOPEMENT

If a young couple didn't have their parents' permission to marry they could choose to elope, running off to Gretna Green in Scotland (where a couple younger than 21 did not need their parents' consent to marry) to be married. This was extremely scandalous behavior and a couple HAD to marry after this or they would be ruined in society forever. We can see the terrible consequences elopement could have in *Pride and Prejudice*, when Lydia runs away with Wickham. Not only does Lydia ruin her own reputation, she also jeopardizes the chances for her sisters to marry well, as no man would want to be associated with this background. Although Wickham and Lydia are made to marry and the scandal somewhat covered up, at the end of the novel Austen does point out the detrimental effect this one decision has had on Lydia's reputation. Another example of elopement occurs in *Mansfield Park*, when Julia runs away with Mr Yates. Although her father condemns this shocking behavior she is saved from some of his wrath by the worse behavior of her sister, who runs away from her husband with another man.

Another option for young couples whose families didn't approve of their relationship was to enter into a secret engagement. Again, although Austen uses this circumstance in her novels she makes clear the moral uncertainty this situation could place one in. We see that Jane Fairfax becomes physically ill from the stress of trying to conceal her engagement to Frank Churchill, and we see the unhappiness Edward suffers from entering into an engagement with a woman he barely knows and who turns out to be completely wrong for him.

Although Jane portrays these other types of courtships in her novels, she uses the less than desirable fates of the characters who pursue these paths to outline the true morals people should be following.

THOSE WHO DIDN'T MARRY

For gentlemen to remain single during this period was not unusual, as many had their own fortune and home. In fact, many only chose to marry much later in life, as we see in *Sense and Sensibility* when the older Colonel Brandon marries Marianne Dashwood.

For women though, remaining single after a certain age carried more of a stigma, and while gentlemen could carry on the same lifestyle as they had followed in their youth, women would enter a new stage of life as a spinster. This was a path that both Jane and Cassandra chose, meaning they became the chaperone aunt, rather than the married mother. The figure of the spinster can be seen in the character of Miss Bates in *Emma*.

In Her Own Words 🌑

As Jane grew older she embraced her role as chaperone to her nieces, once writing to Cassandra 'As I must leave off being young I find many douceurs in being a sort of chaperon, for I am put on the sofa near the fire, and can drink as much wine as I like'.

Of course this option was only open to women who could afford to care for themselves, or who had families to support them. For women who weren't so lucky, one of the only options open to them was to become a governess (see p. 79 for more on this).

🐚 AUSTEN'S ELIGIBLE BACHELORS 🐚

Colonel Brandon

Book: *Sense and Sensibility*

Romantic interest: Marianne Dashwood (although we also hear the story of his ill-fated love affair with Elizabeth Williams).

Who is he?: Colonel Brandon is the Dashwood's neighbor. He takes an interest in Marianne as she reminds him of his first love Elizabeth Williams. At first Marianne thinks that Colonel Brandon is too old to be in love and so doesn't see him in a romantic light. However, after she has suffered her illness after being rejected by Willoughby, she begins to appreciate the Colonel for his romantic, yet realistic tendencies.

Good catch?: Colonel Brandon has extensive property and a large income. He is generally considered to be handsome and is greatly liked by Marianne's family.

Why we love him: Colonel Brandon's story of his lost love makes him very endearing, and the agony he suffers during Marianne's illness proves what a romantic character he is. His caring for Elizabeth's daughter, a child who is not even his own, and the frantic search he conducts when that child goes missing after her affair with Willoughby, make him one of the most dedicated father figures in Austen's novels.

Best moment: The invaluable help he provides in nursing Marianne and bringing her mother from Barton to be with her.

Edward Ferrars

Book: *Sense and Sensibility*

Romantic interest: Elinor Dashwood (although he is engaged to Lucy Steele for most of the novel!).

Who is he?: Edward is the brother of Elinor's sister-in-law Fanny. He and Elinor become close when he is staying at Norwood. When

Lucy Steele confesses that she is secretly engaged to Edward Elinor must conceal her feelings until Lucy marries Edward's brother instead; leaving Edward free to marry the woman he really cares for.

Good catch?: Edward is not described as a handsome man but he is a sensible and caring person who matches Elinor's caring attitude. He doesn't have a large income after he is disinherited but he is given the living on Colonel Brandon's estate.

Why we love him: Edward loves Elinor but does the honorable thing and stands by Lucy Steele when their engagement becomes public, even enduring his mother disowning him and cutting him off. He is perfectly prepared to marry Lucy and support her but he is saved when Lucy manages to snare Edward's now wealthy brother, and he then rushes to propose to Elinor.

Best moment: When Edward reveals he is not married and is finally able to propose to Elinor.

Mr Darcy

Book: *Pride and Prejudice*

Romantic interest: Elizabeth Bennet

Who is he?: Mr Darcy is Mr Bingley's friend. He and Elizabeth first meet at the Meryton Assembly, where he is rude to her and refuses to ask her to dance. Despite his initial rejection of her though, Darcy finds himself drawn to Elizabeth and, fighting his revulsion at her embarrassing family and low connections, he proposes. She vehemently refuses him but as time goes on his efforts to change convince Lizzie she was wrong to judge him so quickly. Both Elizabeth and Darcy realize their mistaken behaviors through their relationship, and when Darcy learns how Elizabeth stood up to Lady Catherine about rumors of their engagement, he rides to Longbourn and confesses that he still loves her.

Good catch?: Darcy is very handsome with a sizeable estate and income. He is very rude at first but he improves as the novel progresses.

Why we love him: Darcy proves to be the real hero of the story when he discovers where Lydia and Wickham are hiding after their elopement, and pays Wickham enough money to convince him to marry Lydia – thereby saving her reputation and her family's. Darcy later tells Elizabeth that everything he did was done out of love for her.

Best moment: When he tells Elizabeth that he still loves her, despite her earlier rejection, and that everything he has done, he has done for her.

Mr Bingley

Book: *Pride and Prejudice*

Romantic interest: Jane Bennet

Who is he?: Mr Bingley becomes the Bennet's neighbor when he rents Netherfield. He immediately shows an interest in Jane, dancing with her several times and paying her great attention but Jane's hopes are dashed when he suddenly goes back to London with no intention of returning. Jane is hurt, but later, when Darcy is trying to make amends for his poor behavior, it turns out that he made Bingley leave Netherfield for fear Jane didn't return his feelings. Bingley soon returns to Longbourn, where he proposes to Jane and is accepted.

Good catch?: Bingley is wealthy, handsome and all of the Bennets adore him.

Why we love him: For being consistently sweet, charming and good natured. He is the perfect match for the kind hearted Jane and he adores her.

Best moment: When he finally works up the courage to propose to Jane, making them both inexpressibly happy.

Edmund Bertram

Book: *Mansfield Park*

Romantic interest: For most of the book Edmund believes himself in love with Mary Crawford, but by the end of the novel he realizes that Fanny Price is his perfect match.

Who is he?: Edmund is Fanny's cousin and becomes Mary's neighbor when she moves into the parsonage at Mansfield Park. Edmund is completely enchanted by the vivacious Mary Crawford but his concern over her disregard for his profession, the church, and her desire for a wealthy husband, means he never manages to profess his feelings. When Edmund finally does decide to propose, Mary expresses a morally repugnant opinion about the affair between her brother and Edmund's sister and they argue, parting on bad terms. Edmund returns to Mansfield to be comforted by Fanny, who has secretly loved him for years. In getting over Mary, Edmund notices Fanny's superiority and finally realizes how much he loves her.

Good catch?: Edmund has a reasonable income and his own property. He is considered handsome and is always kind to Fanny.

Why we love him: Edmund is frustrating to most readers for not realizing how much Fanny cares for him and for his continual blindness to Mary's many faults. But his continuing kindness to Fanny and his eventual realization of Mary's true character mean we respect him for his journey and when he finally realizes he cares for Fanny, it is a real moment of triumph.

Best moment: When Edmund finally realizes that he has always cared for Fanny and in confessing, finds that she has always loved him.

Mr Knightley

Book: *Emma*

Romantic interest: Emma Woodhouse

Who is he?: Mr Knightley is Emma's neighbor and brother-in-law. Emma has known him since she was very young, and he has always chastized her for the selfish or silly behavior which no one else in her family checks her for. They often quarrel but Emma does look to him as her moral compass. Emma has never considered Mr Knightley in a romantic light, but when she worries that he may return Harriet's feelings she suddenly realizes that her panic at the thought of his marrying Harriet arises from her own desire to marry him. When Emma then meets Mr Knightley after she has realized her true feelings, he tries to comfort her over the loss of Frank Churchill but in stating that she never cared for Frank, Mr Knightley confesses that he loves her, and has always loved her.

Good catch?: Mr Knightley is the perfect gentleman in terms of his dancing and manners, and he is also handsome with a large estate and income.

Why we love him: Mr Knightley is the figure of the perfect gentleman in Austen's novels: always kind, caring, and proper. His only fault is his chastising of Emma, but he only does this to improve her character. He is the perfect moral guide for Emma and can only help her become a better person.

Best moment: Although Mr Knightley finally telling Emma he has always loved her may seem his best moment, he tops this by selflessly offering to leave his own home and move in with Emma and her father, so that he and Emma may marry without leaving Mr Woodhouse alone.

Henry Tilney

Book: *Northanger Abbey*

Romantic interest: Catherine Morland

Who is he?: Henry meets Catherine at Bath when he asks the master of ceremonies to introduce him and Catherine is instantly besotted with him. Henry is always kind to Catherine, guiding her in her principles and gently reprimanding her for her silly notions about Gothic novels.

Good catch?: Henry is a charming, handsome young man, who is an excellent dancer and has his own house with a good income.

Why we love him: Henry is always charming and kind, especially to Catherine and his sister. He teases Catherine but he is always patient and tries to lead her in the right direction. Henry shows that he is a true gentleman when he refuses to throw off Catherine as his father orders and stands by her.

Best moment: When Henry tells Catherine how he stood up to his father, faced his anger and his threats to cut him off, all so that he could honor his blossoming relationship with her, and come to Fullerton to propose to her.

Captain Wentworth

Book: *Persuasion*

Romantic interest: Anne Elliot

Who is he?: Captain Wentworth is Anne's former fiancé, whom she hasn't seen for seven years since she broke off their engagement on the advice of her friend Lady Russell. Anne is thrown into Captain Wentworth's company again when his sister- and brother-in-law rent Anne's home. For most of the novel Anne is forced to witness Captain Wentworth flirting with other women, but in being so much together and hearing Anne's views on the constancy of love, he realizes that he still loves her.

Good catch?: Captain Wentworth is a very handsome man who has made a large fortune in the war.

Why we love him: Although Captain Wentworth tries to ignore Anne, he cannot help being kind to her and it is obvious that he still loves her despite the pain she caused him. Captain Wentworth also proves himself a hero when he helps Anne's friend Mrs Smith recover her lost fortune.

Best moment: The letter he writes to Anne confessing his continued love, and their renewed engagement as a result of this letter.

THE MEN WHO GET IN THE WAY

John Willoughby

Book: *Sense and Sensibility*

Lady he tries to lead astray: Marianne Dashwood

Why he is tempting: Willoughby is very open about his feelings for Marianne, constantly dancing with her and taking her for rides in his carriage. He even takes a lock of her hair to keep. It seems certain that they are engaged but when he goes to London, Marianne hears nothing from him and in London he snubs her company, soon after revealing he is engaged to another woman.

How he is discovered: Willoughby is discovered to be a scoundrel when Colonel Brandon reveals that Willoughby has seduced his ward Eliza and abandoned her when she fell pregnant. Willoughby is then cut off by his wealthy aunt, and he goes to London so that he can marry a wealthy heiress.

How he ends up: Willoughby ends up married to a wealthy but cruel wife, and later learns that if he had acted honorably towards Eliza his aunt would have forgiven him, leaving him free to marry Marianne.

George Wickham

Book: *Pride and Prejudice*

Lady he tries to lead astray: Wickham first pays his attentions to Elizabeth Bennet and ruins her opinion of Darcy with his lies, but he eventually leads Lydia astray by eloping with her.

Why he is tempting: Wickham endears himself to people with his charming manners and with his sad tale of how Darcy refused to give him the living he had been promised by Darcy's father, leaving him poor and forcing him to join the militia.

How he is discovered: Elizabeth discovers that Wickham is a liar when Darcy writes to her, explaining the true chain of events: that Wickham refused the living and asked for money instead. When he spent this and was refused more money he tried to seduce Darcy's sister, but Darcy discovered their plot to elope and Wickham fled, leaving Georgiana broken hearted. Elizabeth knows he is a liar but Wickham proves himself to be a real scoundrel when he runs away with Lydia, and only agrees to marry her when Darcy offers him a large sum of money and a commission in the army.

How he ends up: Wickham ends up married to Lydia, a woman he doesn't really care for, and when they constantly live beyond their means he ends up resenting Lydia.

Henry Crawford

Book: *Mansfield Park*

Lady he tries to lead astray: Maria Bertram (and he succeeds!)

Why he is tempting: Henry is a charming young man who flirts with women to make them fall in love with him. He targets Maria

Bertram because she is engaged and succeeds in winning her attentions. When Sir Thomas returns home Henry flees, meaning Maria marries her fiancé out of spite. Henry also tries to win Fanny over but in doing so genuinely falls in love with her.

How he is discovered: Henry does succeed in becoming a better man and almost wins Fanny when his vanity ruins him. He meets with Maria, now married, and his pride is so hurt that she hates him that he decides to try to win her again. In doing so their affair is discovered, and Maria leaves her husband for Henry.

How he ends up: Henry ends up with Maria but refuses to marry her. They become resentful of one another and she eventually leaves him. Henry is left alone with the knowledge that if he had resisted his vanity he would have eventually won Fanny.

Frank Churchill
Book: *Emma*

Lady he tries to lead astray: Emma Woodhouse (but only as a distraction from the fact that he has already convinced Jane Fairfax to enter into a secret engagement).

Why he is tempting: Frank is a vivacious and charming young man who pays his attentions to Emma from the moment he arrives in Highbury.

How he is discovered: Frank is discovered to have been using his flirtation with Emma to cover up his engagement to Jane, when he confesses to the engagement after the death of his wealthy aunt. Frank manages to redeem himself slightly in the apologetic letter he writes to Mrs Weston.

How he ends up: Frank is lucky in that he ends up marrying a woman who will hopefully improve his selfish tendencies.

John Thorpe
Book: *Northanger Abbey*

Lady he tries to lead astray: Catherine Morland

Why he is tempting: Catherine does not find John charming at all, but he pushes himself into her life by making arrangements for her, lying to her and canceling her other arrangements with the Tilneys. It is John who lies to General Tilney about Catherine's wealth and then later makes out she is destitute. Catherine is not led astray by John but he does have a negative impact on her life.

How he is discovered: Catherine is aware of John's controlling behavior from the beginning but is not until the end of the novel that she discovers the role he has played in deceiving the General about her inheritance.

How he ends up: John ends up bitter after Catherine's rejection of his advances, and we hear no more of him after we learn about his lying to the General.

William Elliot

Book: *Persuasion*

Lady he tries to lead astray: Anne Elliot

Why he is tempting: Having been estranged from his family for years, Mr Elliot is suddenly very attentive and charming, to Anne in particular. He makes it clear that he wishes to marry Anne and while she is unsure her greatest incentive for accepting his advances is that it would allow her to follow her beloved mother as Lady Elliot of Kellynch Hall.

How he is discovered: Mr Elliot is discovered to be a scoundrel when Anne's friend Mrs Smith reveals his true character. Mr Elliot ruined her husband Mr Smith, leaving her deeply in debt after his death and refusing to help her. Mrs Smith tells Anne that now that he is wealthy, Mr Elliot only desires to obtain the title of Sir William and has even offered to keep Mrs Clay as his mistress so that she won't marry Sir Walter and give him a son and heir.

How he ends up: When Mr Elliot learns that Anne is engaged once more to Captain Wentworth, he promptly leaves Bath and is last seen in London with Mrs Clay, whom Anne suspects he will marry himself to ensure he receives his inherited title.

🐚 AUSTEN'S LEADING LADIES 🐚

Elinor Dashwood

Book: *Sense and Sensibility*

Romantic interest: Edward Ferrars

Romantic journey she goes through: Elinor is forced to hide her feelings for Edward when she learns that he is secretly engaged to another woman. Elinor has to spend time with this woman and must suppress her own feelings when Lucy constantly talks to her of the engagement and boasts of Edward's attachment to her.

How she wins the man of her dreams: Elinor's superior conduct throughout the novel means that she retains Edward's feelings without ever tempting him to behave dishonorably and break off his engagement. Her conduct is rewarded when Lucy marries Edward's brother instead, and Elinor can accept the man she loves and live happily with him at the parsonage at Delaford.

What we should learn from her: To conduct ourselves in a superior manner even when our own hopes have been dashed.

Marianne Dashwood

Book: *Sense and Sensibility*

Romantic interest: John Willoughby, but she ends up marrying Colonel Brandon

Romantic journey she goes through: Marianne refuses to moderate her displays of her feelings for Willoughby. This ends with the general assumption that she and Willoughby are engaged, which is in fact not actually true. When Willoughby goes to London Marianne doesn't hear any more from him, and when she goes to London he refuses to answer her letters. When they meet at a party he snubs her and the next day returns all of her letters, and it emerges he is engaged to someone else. Marianne is heartbroken and once more gives in to her feelings so much that she succumbs to illness and almost dies. When she recovers she sees the error of her ways and decides to live more sensibly.

How she wins the man of her dreams: Although Marianne doesn't end up with Willoughby, whom she first thought was the man of her dreams, she marries Colonel Brandon who is a much better match for her in terms of an equal and caring relationship.

What we should learn from her: To moderate our feelings and not give in to the excesses of our emotions.

Elizabeth Bennet

Book: *Pride and Prejudice*

Romantic interest: Mr Darcy

Romantic journey she goes through: Elizabeth must learn to overcome her own hurt pride and ill-conceived initial prejudices against Mr Darcy, in order to appreciate his changed character and realize what a perfect partner he is for her.

How she wins the man of her dreams: Elizabeth wins Darcy from the very beginning with her lively behavior and sparkling eyes, but she wins him forever when she forces him to see the error of his ways and improve his character.

What we should learn from her: Elizabeth shows us that we should always reconsider our first impressions and judge people on their current behavior. We should also examine our own conduct before we judge that of others.

Fanny Price

Book: *Mansfield Park*

Romantic interest: Edmund Bertram

Romantic journey she goes through: Fanny has been secretly in love with Edmund for years and is forced to watch him fall in love with Mary Crawford, listening to his praise for her even though Fanny knows he is grossly mistaken about her character. Fanny receives a proposal of marriage from Henry Crawford which everyone encourages her to accept, but despite the appeal of the offer Fanny cannot overlook Henry's moral faults and so refuses his repeated advances.

How she wins the man of her dreams: By staying true to her morals, Fanny proves herself superior to Mary and when Edward finally sees the truth of Mary's character he also sees the superiority of Fanny and realizes what a perfect match she is for him.

What we should learn from her: Fanny's journey illustrates how important it is to remain true to our morals and not give in to tempting offers, even though they may seem the best prospect we have.

Emma Woodhouse

Book: *Emma*

Romantic interest: Mr Knightley

Romantic journey she goes through: Emma must endure Mr Knightley's criticisms of her poor behavior, especially her matchmaking schemes, and even though she fancies herself in love with Frank Churchill, she is so upset at the thought of Mr Knightley marrying someone else that she realizes that she truly loves him.

How she wins the man of her dreams: Although Mr Knightley criticizes Emma, he does it to improve her character and he says he loves her for all of her strengths and how she has borne his judgments.

What we should learn from her: Emma shows us that we should always try to improve our character and not interfere with other people's love lives.

Catherine Morland

Book: *Northanger Abbey*

Romantic interest: Henry Tilney

Romantic journey she goes through: Catherine is besotted with Henry from her first meeting with him and Austen leads her through the typical romantic heroine's journey, worrying when she will next meet him and what his true feelings are. Catherine must suffer the misunderstanding caused by John Thorpe though, meaning Henry's father first courts her affections for Henry and then rejects them. Henry nobly stands by his relationship with Catherine and defies his father to be with her.

How she wins the man of her dreams: Henry first becomes attracted to Catherine because of her feelings for him, but her endearing innocence means he cares for her and decides to stand by her despite his father's anger.

What we should learn from her: Catherine teaches us not to become overwhelmed by the fantastical situations and emotions we find in novels and instead to focus on our real relationships.

Anne Elliot

Book: *Persuasion*

Romantic interest: Captain Wentworth

Romantic journey she goes through: Anne had managed to win her man seven years earlier, but was persuaded that the match was impractical and so gave him up. On meeting with him again Anne has to endure his cold treatment of her and watch him flirting with other women. The more time they spend together though, the more their old feelings emerge and Anne's steadfast dedication to Captain Wentworth results in his confessing that he still loves her.

How she wins the man of her dreams: Although Anne was persuaded to break off her engagement she remains true to Captain Wentworth, turning down promising offers of marriage from other men. It is this constant character and commitment that gives Captain Wentworth the courage to make his offer again.

What we should learn from her: Anne's experiences teach us to be true to our feelings and not to be persuaded into modes of action that deny these feelings.

THE BAD GIRLS

Lucy Steele

Book: *Sense and Sensibility*

Who she flirts with: Lucy is secretly engaged to Edward Ferrars for almost the entire novel, but when their engagement becomes public Edward's mother cuts him off. Lucy clings on to Edward but while he is away trying to set up a home for them, Lucy begins flirting with Edward's brother Robert, who is now set to inherit his mother's entire fortune. Lucy's flattery works on Robert's vanity and he marries Lucy without consulting with his mother.

How her flirtations ruin her: Lucy gets what she wants by marrying a rich man but everyone is shocked at her treatment of Edward, meaning her reputation is ruined.

Lydia Bennet

Book: *Pride and Prejudice*

Who she flirts with: Lydia flirts with all of the officers in the militia but it is Wickham she eventually runs away with.

How her flirtations ruin her: Lydia's reputation is ruined when she runs away with Wickham, and her behavior also threatens the reputation of her family. Their marriage rectifies the matter somewhat, but there is always a tarnish on her name.

Mary Crawford

Book: *Mansfield Park*

Who she flirts with: Mary begins flirting with Tom Bertram, as he is the eldest son and set to inherit. However, she soon becomes more attracted to Edmund and focuses on winning him instead. She is concerned at his choosing to be a clergyman but she is sure she will be able to convince him to have a house in town.

How her flirtations ruin her: Mary's lax moral opinions about the affair between Henry and Maria ruin her chances with Edmund, and her sexually suggestive offer that he stay after their argument only further convinces him to leave off her acquaintance forever. Mary then returns to her quest to find a wealthy husband.

Mrs Elton

Book: *Emma*

Who she flirts with: Mrs Elton enters the novel as Miss Hawkins, a young woman from a 'new money' family determined to land a husband, eventually setting her sights on Mr Elton. Mrs Elton is not so much a flirt, as a woman obsessed with the position her marital status gives her.

How her flirtations ruin her: Mrs Elton's constant boasting and insistence on the pre-eminence given to her by her status as a new wife become very grating to the Hartfield society and to Emma in particular, who cannot stand Mrs Elton's assumption that they are now on the same social level.

Isabella Thorpe
Book: *Northanger Abbey*

Who she flirts with: Isabella first sets her sights on James Morland and even secures an engagement. When the wealthier and dashing Captain Tilney arrives though, Isabella begins to pay more attention to him than to her fiancé.

How her flirtations ruin her: Isabella flirts with Captain Tilney so much that James breaks off their engagement. At this point Captain Tilney also leaves Bath, leaving Isabella with nothing.

Mrs Clay
Book: *Persuasion*

Who she flirts with: Mrs Clay constantly flatters Sir Walter and panders to his every need. She is so successful that Sir Walter even begins to consider her pretty, where before he could never see past her freckles.

How her flirtations ruin her: Both Anne and Lady Russell worry that Mrs Clay will win Sir Walter's affections, and when Mr Elliot joins their company he is also so concerned that he even offers to establish Mrs Clay as his mistress to keep her from marrying Sir Walter. Mrs Clay ruins herself by accepting this offer, and when Mr Elliot's plans to marry Anne fall through, it is even rumored that he is to marry Mrs Clay.

8

'Darcy is the romantic destiny' – Colin Firth: Film and TV adaptations of Austen's novels

Austen's works are not only held as great works of literature, their witty dialogue, intriguing romances and realistic characters have allowed her novels to spawn countless adaptations in both film and television.

Austen's novels contain so much written dialogue that it is easy for filmmakers to reproduce the kind of witty exchanges we see between Darcy and Elizabeth word for word in their productions. Of course some scriptwriters have attempted to reinterpret Austen's work: some have relocated the action to a modern setting (such as *Clueless*); some have made the letters and Austen's social commentary part of the dialogue; and some have even incorporated aspects of Jane's life – for example using the titles of her *Juvenilia* as titles of the books the characters are reading.

Austen's works are also now free of copyright restrictions, meaning her novels are attractive options for film and television producers.

❧ SENSE AND SENSIBILITY ❧

TELEVISION ADAPTATIONS

2008 BBC television adaptation

This BBC television adaptation was aired in 2008 in both the UK and the USA and was made up of a British cast including David Morrissey, Dominic Cooper, Dan Stevens, Mark Williams, Janet McTeer and Mark Gatiss. This three part drama was written by award winning writer Andrew Davies, who also wrote the beloved 1995 BBC adaptation of *Pride and Prejudice*, starring Colin Firth. The series met with favorable reviews, although some critics were unsure of the more overt portrayal of sexual undertones. Davies had intentionally highlighted this aspect, saying he hoped the adaptation was, 'more overtly sexual than most previous Austen adaptations seen on screen and [that it] gets to grips with the dark underbelly of the book'. The series received two Emmy nominations and a Bafta (British Academy of Film and Television Arts) nomination for Best Original Television Music.

Watch for: The excellent script and cast.

. . . But ignore: The overt sexuality (if you think it has no place in Austen!).

Costume trivia

- Lucy Steele (Anna Madeley) wears a pale blue dress with checked trim on the sleeves at Mrs Jennings' house in London – the same dress Emma Thompson wore as Elinor Dashwood in the 1995 film version.

- Marianne Dashwood (Charity Wakefield) wears a brown velvet gown – the same dress worn by Keira Knightley in *Pride and Prejudice* (2005).

Some filming locations

- Blackpool Mill Cottage on the Hartland Abbey Estate in Devon was used as Barton Cottage

- The coastal footpath on the Hartland Abbey Estate in Devon was used as the grounds of Barton Cottage

- Ham House in Richmond, Surrey was used for the interior of Norland and the exterior of Cleveland

- Loseley Park in Guildford was used as the exterior of Barton Park and the library at Delaford

- Wrotham Park in Barnet, Hertfordshire was used as Norland

1971 BBC television adaptation

This adaptation was shown on the BBC in 1971 and contained a strong cast, including Michael Aldridge, Sheila Ballantine, Esme Church, Joanna David as Elinor Dashwood (who also plays Mrs Gardiner in the 1995 adaptation of *Pride and Prejudice*), Isabel Dean, Robin Ellis, Clive Francis, Ciaran Madden, Richard Owens, Patricia Routledge and Jo Kendall.

Watch for: The accurate portrayal of the cruel treatment Lucy Steele submits Elinor to.

. . . But ignore: The incongruous 1970s hairstyles and the fact that Eliza Williams is Colonel Brandon's niece, making his secrecy about her identity seem ridiculous.

1981 BBC television adaptation

This seven part adaptation was broadcast on the BBC in 1981 and while its length means it contains more scenes from the novel than most adaptations, it makes one major change in its deletion of the character of Margaret Dashwood. The director and screenwriter also add in scenes of dialogue (making Edward's true feelings for Elinor more evident for example), and even alter Marianne's first meeting with Willoughby to take place on a sunny day rather than during a rainstorm. The cast includes Irene Richard (Elinor Dashwood), Tracey Childs (Marianne Dashwood), Diana Fairfax (Mrs Dashwood), Peter Gale (John Dashwood), Amanda Boxer (Fanny Dashwood), and Bosco Hogan (Edward Ferrars).

Watch for: The totality of scenes from the novel.

. . . But ignore: The glaring liberties taken with settings and the character list.

Some filming locations

- Babington House in Somerset served as Norland

- Came Cottage in Dorchester was used as Barton Cottage

- Came Park was used as Barton Park

FILM ADAPTATIONS

1996 film adaptation

This 1996 film version of Austen's novel was directed by Ang Lee, with a screenplay written by Emma Thompson – who also plays the part of Elinor Dashwood. Thompson won an Oscar for Best Screenplay and a Bafta for Best Actress for this film. The film also won Best Film at the Baftas and Best Supporting Actress for Kate Winslet, who plays Marianne. Thompson was praised for her adaptation of Austen's novel, as she retains a great sense of the contrast between Marianne and Elinor's characters but still portrays them as loving sisters. This is perhaps one of the best known adaptations of *Sense and Sensibility* and is a must for any Austen fan.

The film has an all-star cast, including Hugh Grant as Edward Ferrars, Alan Rickman as Colonel Brandon and Hugh Laurie as Mr Palmer. Thompson had originally wanted sisters Joely and Natasha Richardson to play the Dashwood sisters, but when Ang Lee insisted that she play the role of Elinor, Thompson was forced to increase Elinor's age from 19 to 27.

Watch for: Thompson's wonderful script and the fantastic sisterly portrayal by Kate Winslet and Emma Thompson.

. . . But ignore: The fact that during the film Marianne quotes the line, 'Is love a fancy or a feeling', the first line of a sonnet written by Samuel Taylor Coleridge's son, Hartley Coleridge. The only problem is this sonnet was written in the 1830s, almost 20 years after the period and publication of *Sense and Sensibility*.

Pocket Fact ⚓

Director Ang Lee had never read the novel when the film studio approached him with Emma Thompson's script.

Costume trivia

Hugh Laurie wears a green and cream waistcoat in the film, which was also worn by Mr Bennet in a 1995 version of *Pride and Prejudice*, and by James McAvoy as Tom Lefroy in *Becoming Jane*.

Some filming locations

- Berry Pomeroy Church in Devon is where Marianne and Colonel Brandon are married

- Compton Castle in Paignton serves as Combe Magna

- Efford House in Plymouth serves as Barton Cottage

- Trafalgar Park in Wiltshire serves as Barton Park

🐚 *PRIDE AND PREJUDICE* 🐚

TELEVISION ADAPTATIONS

1980 BBC adaptation

This five part adaptation appeared on British screens in 1980 and was written by the novelist Fay Weldon. The series was later broadcast in the US in 1981.

Watch for: A great portrayal of Elizabeth Bennet by Elizabeth Garvie and an extremely accurate script by Fay Weldon.

. . . But ignore: The scene in the assembly hall dance where one of the musicians is seen to be playing a concertina. Unfortunately concertinas were not invented until the 1820s, about 20 years later than the time period of the novel.

Costume trivia

- The beige dress with a paisley bodice that Sabina Franklyn (Jane Bennet) wears at Longbourn, is also worn by a guest at Fanny's wedding in *Miss Austen Regrets* (2008).

- Jennifer Granville, who plays Mrs Hurst, wears a pale blue gown with a gold-flowered bodice on Elizabeth's first evening at Netherfield. This gown is also worn by Doran Goodwin as Emma at the Randalls' Christmas Party in the 1972 adaptation of *Emma*, and is also worn by a guest at Fanny's ball in the 1983 adaptation of *Mansfield Park*.

Some filming locations

- Renishaw Hall in Derbyshire serves as Pemberley

- Thorpe Tilney Hall in Lincolnshire serves as Longbourn
- Well Vale in Alford, Lincolnshire, serves as Netherfield

Pocket Fact 🔱

When discussing her screenplay for the series, Fay Weldon said, 'I hope it makes Pride and Prejudice *accessible to those who might never have read the book and pleasurable for those who know it well.'*

1995 BBC adaptation

This six part adaptation of *Pride and Prejudice* is perhaps the best known, and certainly the most beloved for introducing Colin Firth as Mr Darcy. The BBC made this adaptation with funding from the American A&E Network. The series was shown in six parts in the UK in 1995 and was shown over three consecutive nights as double episodes in the US in 1996. The final episode was watched by over 10 million viewers in the UK and the video version of the series had sold out twice before the last episode had even been aired. The cast includes many promising British actors including, of course, Colin Firth as Mr Darcy, Jennifer Ehle as Elizabeth, Alison Steadman as Mrs Bennet, a young Crispin Bonham Carter as Bingley and Julia Sawalha as Lydia.

The series was hugely popular, with the media discussing everything from period wallpaper to how wealthy the Darcy family would be in modern times. The off-screen romance between Colin Firth and Jennifer Ehle also caused a media stir but sadly for Austen fans it didn't last. Many viewers are also disappointed to learn that their favorite scene of Darcy emerging from a swim in the lake in a dripping wet white shirt is, sadly, not present in Austen's novel.

Pocket Fact 🔱

The BBC auctioned one of Colin Firth's famous shirts for charity, telling women it was their chance to take, 'a last look at the shirt they longed to undo'.

The series received Bafta nominations for Best Drama Serial, Best Costume Drama and Best Hair and Make Up. Jennifer Ehle won the Bafta for Best Actress, while Colin Firth won the Broadcasting Press Guild Award for Best Actor. The series also won an Emmy for Outstanding Individual Achievement in Costume Drama, and was nominated in several other categories.

Watch for: The fantastic development of the relationship between Darcy and Elizabeth, and the numerous scenes from the novel that are included.

. . . But ignore: Don't ignore the lake scene but try not to let it distract you from the rest of the series!

Mr Darcy madness

This was the adaptation which launched Mr Darcy, and particularly Colin Firth, as a sex symbol. The scene where he emerges from the lake in his dripping wet white shirt has been named one of the most unforgettable moments in British TV. It is hard to believe that Firth had refused the role at first, believing he wasn't right for the part. Only director Sur Birtwistle's persistence persuaded him to accept.

When filming that famous scene it was actually a stuntman who dove into the lake at Lyme Park in Cheshire (being used as Pemberley) because there was a risk of catching Weil's disease from the water. Colin Firth shot his underwater scenes at the Ealing Studios in London.

The lake scene has taken on a life of its own, now following Colin Firth throughout his career. Richard Curtis made fun of the scene in Love Actually *by having Firth's character fall in a lake, and the scene was also copied in Firth's role in* St Trinian's. *The TV series* Lost in Austen *also gave its nod to the iconic moment when the modern day heroine convinces Mr Darcy to recreate the scene for her.*

Pocket Fact

Anna Chancellor, who plays the haughty Caroline Bingley, is actually Jane Austen's niece; she is a direct descendant of Jane's brother Edward.

Costume trivia

- The green-striped gown with velvet Spencer jacket Anna Chancellor (Caroline Bingley) wears at Netherfield Hall, is the same costume worn by Julia Davis (Elizabeth Elliot) at Kellynch Hall in *Persuasion* (2007).

- The green and beige patterned waistcoat Benjamin Whitrow (Mr Bennet) wears at Longbourn is the same costume James McAvoy (Tom Lefroy) wears to Lady Gresham's ball in *Becoming Jane* (2007). The costume is also worn by Hugh Laurie (Mr Palmer) at the London ball in *Sense and Sensibility* (1995) and by Jonny Lee Miller (Mr Knightley) for the strawberry-picking party in *Emma* (2009).

Some filming locations

- Belton House in Lincolnshire serves as Rosings

- Lacock Abbey serves as Pemberley interiors

- Lyme Park in Cheshire serves as Pemberley exterior

FILM ADAPTATIONS

1940 film adaptation

This Hollywood adaptation of Jane Austen's novel starred Laurence Olivier as Darcy, Greer Garson as Elizabeth Bennet and was written by Aldous Huxley, who based the script on a stage adaptation rather than the novel itself. The film is set in the Victorian era, much later than Austen's original setting. This change was brought about by a decision to re-use the flamboyant costumes from *Gone With the Wind*, which would have been out of place in the novel's original setting. The film was critically well received, as aside from the period change and a major alteration to the argument between Lizzy and Lady Catherine, the film is very true to the novel and both Olivier and Greer won praise for their performances. The film won an Academy Award for Best Art Direction.

Watch for: The brilliant portrayals by both Olivier and Greer.

. . . But ignore: The incongruous costumes and period change.

Pocket Fact ⚱

It wasn't only the costumes that were totally out of keeping with Austen's original novel. Following the screwball comedy style popular at the time, the tagline for the film wasn't some of Austen's inspired prose, but instead a line which read, 'Bachelors beware! Five gorgeous beauties are on a madcap manhunt!'

Costume trivia

MGM decided to re-use the costumes from *Gone With the Wind* for budgetary reasons, although only the extras wore recycled costumes. The lead characters were all given new creations.

2005 film adaptation

This most recent adaptation of the novel was directed by Joe Wright, and starred Keira Knightley as Lizzie, Rosamund Pike as Jane, Donald Sutherland as Mr Bennet, Brenda Blethyn as Mrs Bennet and Matthew Macfadyen as Darcy. The adaptation was well received, although some claim that no adaptation will ever live up to the 1995 BBC television version. The film had a different ending in the US: a scene featuring Darcy and Lizzy as Mrs Darcy, discussing how happy they are. This ending did not test well with British audiences though and was cut for the UK release. The film does stay true to the book, although its reduced length means that many scenes and characters are cut and some events are compressed in terms of time. Critics praised Keira Knightley for her performance but Macfadyen received mixed reviews: some praised his more sensitive portrayal of the character than Colin Firth, while others said he lacked emotional development.

Pocket Fact ⚜

Joe Wright was not initially keen on Keira Knightley as he thought she would be too attractive for the part. He changed his mind upon meeting her, deciding her tomboyish attitude would be perfect for the feisty Elizabeth Bennet.

Keira Knightley received both an Oscar nomination and a Golden Globe for Best Actress for her portrayal of Lizzy, and the film was also nominated for Best Original Score, Best Art Direction and Best Costume Design. The film received several Bafta nominations and director Joe Wright won the award for Most Promising Newcomer.

Watch for: The fantastic cinematography and scenery.

. . . But ignore: The urge to compare Matthew Macfadyen's Mr Darcy to Colin Firth's: just enjoy his portrayal in its own right.

Some filming locations

- Chatsworth house in Derbyshire serves as Pemberley

- Groombridge Place in Kent serves as Longbourn

- The Temple of Apollo in Stourhead Garden, Warminster, Wiltshire is the scene of Darcy's first proposal

Pocket Fact ♆

At the beginning of the movie, Elizabeth is shown reading a novel called First Impressions, the original title of Pride and Prejudice.

🐚 MANSFIELD PARK 🐚

TELEVISION ADAPTATIONS

1983 BBC adaptation

This BBC adaptation of Mansfield Park was aired in 1983, and featured a British cast including a very shy and nervous portrayal of Fanny by Sylvestra Le Touzel. This adaptation remains very true to the novel, perhaps making it slightly less exciting than other adaptations.

This production may seem dated and slow to modern audiences but does offer a great insight into the novel – particularly the appealing nature of the Crawfords' liberal behavior, which brings life and fun to Mansfield Park, although not being totally morally acceptable. This adaptation also plays up the Cinderella-like apsects of Fannys' life in a bid to make her more sympathetic.

Watch for: The insight the accurate script gives to the appeal of the Crawfords' morally ambiguous behavior.

. . . But ignore: Those aspects of Le Touzel's portrayal that make Fanny seem boring and inexplicably frightened.

Costume trivia

- The brown gown with red and blue dots worn by Mary Crawford is also worn by Caroline Bingley in *Lost in Austen*.

- The striped mauve dress Mrs Norris wears, is also worn by Mrs Weston in the 1996 TV adaptation of *Emma* and by Mrs Martin in the 2009 TV adaptation of *Emma*.

Some filming locations

- Brympton d'Evercy, Yeovil, Somerset serves as Sotherton Court

- Somerley, Ringwood, Hampshire serves as Mansfield Park

Pocket Fact ⚘

The actor Jonny Lee Miller appears in this adaptation as Fanny's younger brother Charles. He later appears in the 1999 film version as Edmund Bertram.

2007 ITV adaptation

This 2007 television adaptation of Mansfield Park was made by the British TV network ITV as part of their Jane Austen season. The drama is two hours long and was also broadcast in the US and Canada. The adaptation had quite a famous cast with Billie Piper as Fanny, Blake Ritson as Edmund, Michelle Ryan as Maria Bertram and James D'Arcy as Tom Bertram.

The adaptation did not meet with favorable reviews as it was felt that the script had lost all of Austen's wit and clever turn of phrase, and the choice of Billie Piper for the timid Fanny Price was criticized. Clearly budget and length were a constriction for this adaptation as all of the action takes place in one location (Newby Hall in North Yorkshire), with the ball thrown in Fanny's honor being replaced by a picnic and her trip to Portsmouth replaced with the family going away and leaving her at Mansfield alone. These omissions are to the detriment of the story and only add to the lackluster appeal of this adaptation.

Watch for: The celebrity cast.

. . . But ignore: The poor script.

FILM ADAPTATIONS

1999 film adaptation

This film version of the novel was made by MGM and released in 1999, making its debut at the Montreal Film Festival. Directed by

Patricia Rozema, who also wrote the screenplay, the cast features both British and American actors, including Frances O' Connor as Fanny, Jonny Lee Miller as Edmund, James Purefoy as Tom Bertram and Harold Pinter as Sir Thomas Bertram. The film chooses to play up some of the main themes found in the novel, such as the issue of slavery. This is given much more focus than in the novel, with the ill treatment of slaves on Sir Thomas' estate in Antigua being frequently referred to. The character of Fanny is also changed significantly, being shown as less physically weak, and much more confident and outspoken. She is also often shown writing, and one of these works, entitled *The History of the World*, is the title of a piece written by Jane Austen in her youth. The adaptation also makes some key plot changes, including the removal of the character of Fanny's brother William, and Fanny accepting Henry Crawford's proposal only to reject it the next day; another hint at Austen's own experience as she had done this to a suitor when she was younger.

Watch for: A winning (if slightly inaccurate) portrayal of Fanny by Frances O Connor.

. . . But ignore: The exaggerated political aspects of slavery, mentioned only briefly in the novel.

Pocket Fact 🕯

After filming wrapped, the production team left behind a flock of doves used in a scene shot in Charlestown in Cornwall. The birds survived thanks to a local woman, who fed them fearing they wouldn't be able to compete against the local seagulls.

Costume trivia
Lady Bertram wears a brown gown with a white muslin overdress, the same dress worn by Jennifer Ehle in the 1995 BBC adaptation of *Pride and Prejudice*.

Pocket Fact 📖

Victoria Hamilton, who plays Maria Bertram, also appears in the 1995 adaptation of Pride and Prejudice *as Mrs Foster, and in a 1995 adaptation of* Persuasion *as Henrietta Musgrove.*

Some filming locations

- Charlestown, Cornwall serves as Portsmouth

- Kirby Hall, Corby, Northamptonshire serves as Mansfield Park

🐚 *EMMA* 🐚

TELEVISION ADAPTATIONS

1972 BBC adaptation

The BBC broadcast this adaptation with Doran Godwin as Emma, John Carson as Mr Knightley and Debbie Bowen as Harriet Smith in 1972. It has been called one of the best early Austen adaptations done by the BBC and its six parts are long enough to cover all the events of the novel. This adaptation is well cast and the costumes were thoroughly researched to reflect the fashion of the time. This adaptation is perfect to gain a full understanding of the novel.

Watch for: Its full portrayal of the novel – great for getting to grips with the entirety of the book.

. . . But ignore: The fact that most of the cast are much older than the characters they are playing. A 30-something Doran Godwin is playing 20 year old Emma!

Costume trivia

- Jane Fairfax wears a floral gown which was previously worn by the actress who played Marianne in the 1971 adaptation of *Sense and Sensibility*.

- Emma wears a blue gown to the Christmas party at Randalls, the same dress worn by Mrs Hurst in *Pride and Prejudice* (1980) and by a guest at Fanny's ball in *Mansfield Park* (1983).

2009 BBC adaptation

This four part adaptation was written by Sandy Welch, who had previously written other costume dramas including a version of *Jane Eyre*. The cast included Romola Garai as Emma, Jonny Lee Miller as Mr Knightley, Michael Gambon as Mr Woodhouse and Louise Dylan as Harriet Smith. The series was filmed over a four day period in Chilham, a village in Kent. The crew had to cover modern road markings with gravel, and filming took place every day between 8am and 7pm during the school vacation to minimize the disruption to village life.

The adaptation received mixed reviews, with praise for Romola Garai and Michael Gambon, but some felt Jonny Lee Miller played Mr Knightley too much like a 'bad boy' and that the narration became too obtrusive in the final episodes. The adaptation lost viewers on a weekly basis, which some say spells, 'the end of the bonnet and bustle', but which others blamed on the competition from the TV talent show *X Factor* which aired at the same time.

Watch for: The length of the series meant it could include many scenes from the novel and accurately reflect the slow pace of life in Highbury.

. . . But ignore: Jonny Lee Miller trying to make Mr Knightley into a bad boy.

Some filming locations

- 6 Fitzroy Square, Bloomsbury, served as John Knightley's London house

- Chilham, Kent served as the village of Highbury

- Loseley Park, Guildford, Surrey serves as Donwell Abbey, Mr Knightley's estate

Pocket Fact ⚜

The script for this adaptation was originally commissioned in 1995 but as Miramax and Meridien were also producing adaptations of Emma *that year, the project was put on hold for more than a decade.*

1996 TV movie adaptation

This made-for-television adaptation was made in the same year as the Gywneth Paltrow film version by A&E productions. Andrew Davies, who had written the screenplay for the 1995 adaptation of *Pride and Prejudice*, wrote this adaptation which was aired in 1996, and aired again on ITV in 2007 as part of their Jane Austen season. Kate Beckinsale takes on the role of Emma, with Mark Strong as Mr Knightley and Samantha Morton as Harriet Smith. The adaptation won two Emmys for Art Direction and Costume Design, and critics praised Davies' screenplay as being faithful to the novel.

Watch for: The fantastic costumes and faithful screenplay.

. . . But ignore: How short the film is.

Costume trivia

- Mrs Weston wears a pink dress which had previously been worn by Jane Bennet in the 1995 adaptation of *Pride and Prejudice*.

- Jane Fairfax wears a turquoise pelisse which had been worn by Georgiana Darcy in the 1995 *Pride and Prejudice* and later by Lucy Steele in the 2008 *Sense and Sensibility*.

- Harriet Smith wears a bonnet with blue trimming which has also been worn in the 2007 adaptation of *Persuasion* by Louisa Musgrove.

Some filming locations

- Lacock, Wiltshire served as Highbury Village

- Stanway House, Stow-on-the-Wold, Gloucestershire served as Donwell Abbey

- Trafalgar Park, North Salisbury, Wiltshire served as Hartfield

Pocket Fact 🔱

There is currently a Bollywood version of Emma *being shot in Delhi, entitled* Aisha.

FILM ADAPTATIONS

1996 film adaptation

This film version of *Emma* was directed by Douglas McGrath, who also wrote the screenplay, and was released by Miramax in 1996. The film features an all star cast including Gywneth Paltrow as Emma, Alan Cumming as Mr Elton, Toni Collete as Harriet Smith, Jeremy Northam as Mr Knightley and Ewan McGregor as Frank Churchill. Gywneth Paltrow won great praise for her part, particularly for her English accent, which convincingly covered her native American tones. The film won an Oscar for Best Music and was nominated for Best Costume Design. This adaptation stays close to the plot of the novel but does play up the friendly banter between Emma and Knightley to make their relationship more interesting.

Watch for: Paltrow's convincing accent as Emma surrounded by lush, extravagant English countryside shots.

. . . *But ignore:* Ewan McGregor's terrible wig.

Some filming locations

- Came House, Dorchester, Dorset served as Hartfield

- Claydon House, Middle Claydon, Buckinghamshire served as Donwell Abbey

- Evershot, Dorset served as Highbury village

Pocket Fact 🕎

The mother and daughter team of Mrs and Miss Bates is played by real life mother and daughter Phyllida Law and Sophie Thompson, the mother and sister of Emma Thompson.

🐚 NORTHANGER ABBEY 🐚

TELEVISION ADAPTATIONS

1986 BBC adaptation

This adaptation was another joint venture between the BBC and A&E network. The adaptation stars Katherine Schlesinger as Catherine Morland and Peter Firth as Henry Tilney. The adaptation did not receive good reviews, as many critics felt it had missed the point of Austen's satire – praising the Gothic elements of the story that should have been ridiculed. The costumes and settings for the film were praised though.

Watch for: The luxurious costumes and authentic Bath locations.

. . . *But ignore:* The blatant misunderstanding of Austen's satire.

Costume trivia

Mrs Morland wears a striped muslin dress which has also been worn in the 1996 adaptation of *Emma* by Harriet Smith, by Susan Price in the 1999 *Mansfield Park*, and by Marianne in the 2008 *Sense and Sensibility*.

Some filming locations

- Bodiam Castle, Bodiam, East Sussex served as Northanger Abbey

- Number One, Royal Crescent, Bath served as the Allens' Bath lodgings

2007 ITV adaptation

This adaptation was produced by ITV, again as part of their Jane Austen season, written by veteran Austen screen writer

Andrew Davies. The series was just two hours long and was shown in both the UK and the US. The cast included Felicity Jones as Catherine, JJ Field as Henry Tilney and Carey Mulligan as Isabella Thorpe. Sylvestra Le Touzel, who played Fanny Price in the 1983 adaptation of *Mansfield Park*, appeared as Mrs Allen. Although the novel is heavily abridged, Davies does this tastefully without losing any of Austen's style or any major plot devices, and it serves as a good adaptation of a neglected work. The series was shot almost entirely in Ireland, despite the centrality of Bath as a setting for the novel.

Watch for: A short presentation which still manages to capture the essence of Austen's novels.

. . . *But ignore:* The Irish locations in place of Bath.

Pocket Fact ⚓

Northanger Abbey *has only been made into two adaptations.*

Costume trivia

- Henry Tilney wears a green coat, which had also been worn by Colin Firth as Mr Darcy in the 1995 adaptation of *Pride and Prejudice*.

- Catherine Morland wears a straw bonnet, which appeared in the 2005 *Pride and Prejudice* when it was worn by Charlotte Lucas.

Some filming locations

- Ardbraccan House in County Meath served as Fullerton church and rectory

- King's Inns in Henrietta Street in Dublin, featured as Bath

- Lismore Castle, in County Waterford, served as Northanger Abbey

❧ *PERSUASION* ❧

TELEVISION ADAPTATIONS

1971 BBC adaptation

This two part series was made by Granada for the BBC and was broadcast in 1971. It starred Ann Firbank as Anne Elliot and Bryan Marshall as Captain Wentworth. The series has been praised for being very true to the novel, containing key scenes and passages, and keeping the characters close to those found in Austen's novel – not exaggerated caricatures as seen in some other adaptations.

Watch for: The accurate script containing many key scenes.

. . . But ignore: The World War Two tank traps which are visible when Anne and Captain Wentworth walk down the country lane.

Some filming locations

- Frampton Court, Frampton-on-Severn, Gloucestershire served as Uppercross

- The Orangery, Frampton Court, Frampton-on-Severn, Gloucestershire served as Kellynch lodge

1995 BBC adaptation

This adaptation was broadcast on the BBC in 1995 and was later released in movie theater's in the US. It was directed by theater director Roger Mitchell and starred Amanda Root as Anne and Ciaran Hinds as Captain Wentworth. The film was critically acclaimed and received several Bafta awards including Best Costume Design, Best Design, Best Music and Best Single Drama. This adaptation stays true to the novel, conveying the complicated love affair between Anne and Captain Wentworth very well and aptly portraying the society of the Napoleonic era in which the novel takes place. One departure from traditional Austen is the public kiss that takes place between Anne and Captain Wentworth at the end: the media made much of this controversial moment but it simply serves to dramatize the reunion of the two lovers after eight long years. The series was shot entirely on location in Bath, and only used natural light.

Watch for: The fantastic interaction between Root and Hinds as Anne and Captain Wentworth, as well as the beautiful Bath settings.

. . . But ignore: The fact that Austen would probably have disapproved of the public kiss at the end.

Costume trivia

The green Spencer (see glossary) that Amanda Root wears as Anne Elliot is worn by Sally Hawkins to play the same part in the 2007 adaptation.

Some filming locations

- Barnsley Park, Barnsley, Gloucestershire served as Kellynch Hall

- Bath, Somerset

- Sheldon Manor, Chippenham, Wiltshire served as Uppercross

Pocket Fact 🔱

The closing shots of Captain Wentworth's ship are actually borrowed from the 1984 film The Bounty, *as the budget wouldn't allow for such extravagant shots.*

2007 ITV adaptation

Another part of ITV's Jane Austen season, this film was shot entirely on location in Bath, Lyme and Dorset and was broadcast in 2007. The film was directed by Adrian Shergold, who won a Bafta for best director, Sally Hawkins as Anne Elliot (who won a Royal Television Society Award) and Rupert Penry-Jones. The cast also features Anthony Head as Sir Walter.

Watch for: The genuine Bath locations and fantastic performances from a brilliant British cast.

. . . But ignore: The scene where Anne is running through the streets of Bath, right before she bumps into Charles and Captain Wentworth, and a radio tower can be seen in the background.

Costume trivia

Henrietta Musgrove wears a white gown with black dots that had previously been seen on Jane Bennet in the 1995 *Pride and Prejudice* and on Jane Fairfax in the 1996 *Emma*.

Some filming locations

- Assembly Rooms, Bath, Somerset

- Lyme Regis, Dorset

- Neston Park, Corsham, Wiltshire served as Kellynch Hall and the interior of Camden Place

- Sheldon Manor, Chippenham, Wiltshire served as Uppercross

🦪 MODERN DAY RETELLINGS 🦪

Jane's novels have inspired countless period dramas in both television and film, which use her works almost verbatim and try to follow her novels closely to reproduce the story. However, the intricate stories Austen weaves, and the compelling characters she creates, have also inspired writers to imagine the events of her novels in the modern day, or in different cultures, giving new life to her beloved works.

BRIDGET JONES'S DIARY

Helen Fielding's novels about a 30-something single girl trying to find her own Mr Darcy are loosely based on *Pride and Prejudice*. Fielding also admits that the relationship between Darcy and Elizabeth in the 1995 BBC adaptation provided huge inspiration for her when she was turning her newspaper column about Bridget into the novel. Following the success of the novels, a film version of *Bridget Jones's Diary* was released in 2001, starring Renee Zellwegger as Bridget, Hugh Grant as the scoundrel Daniel Cleaver and Colin Firth as Mark Darcy. The film follows Bridget as she worries about her weight and her love life.

There was some concern at the thought of Texan Renee playing a British heroine, but her impeccable accent (and willingness to gain 20lb for the part) proved critics wrong and gained her an

Academy Award nomination. The film retains its links to *Pride and Prejudice* not only in the story-line but also in some subtle hints. For example, the name of the publishing company where Bridget works is 'Pemberley Press', and the film's voiceover features the line, 'It is a truth universally acknowledged that when one part of your life starts looking up, another part falls to pieces' – a modern interpretation of Austen's most famous opening line.

Pocket Fact 🔱

During filming Renee Zellwegger worked at a publishing company in London to perfect her accent. It is claimed that some of her colleagues didn't recognize her and were puzzled by the fact that she kept a picture of Jim Carrey (her boyfriend at the time) on her desk.

BRIDE AND PREJUDICE

This 2004 film saw Bollywood fuse with Austen, as *Pride and Prejudice* is told Bollywood style, complete with singing and dancing. The story follows that of the novel closely, with Mrs Bashki looking for husbands for her daughters, and just a few changes to character names – we see Lalita becoming romantically entangled with the handsome William Darcy. The lead actress in the film, Aishwarya Rai, decided not to read *Pride and Prejudice* before the filming so that she wouldn't be influenced by the character of Elizabeth Bennet.

CLUELESS

Amy Heckerling's 1995 film transports Jane Austen's *Emma* to Beverley Hills and renames her heroine Cher. The character and events of the film remain largely the same as the 1815 novel, despite their new location of an American high school rather than a small English village. Cher is a superficial but well meaning girl who plays match-maker for her two teachers, and adopts the new girl Tai as her makeover project. Cher is constantly criticized by her step-brother Josh, whom Cher eventually realizes she is in love with. The film has become a cult classic and even inspired a TV series and a series of books.

Pocket Fact 💡

When film studio Paramount asked Amy Heckerling to write a film for teenagers, she instantly thought of Emma *– a book she had read and loved as a teenager.*

METROPOLITAN

The 1990 film *Metropolitan* is actually a loose adaptation of *Mansfield Park*. Written and directed by Whit Stillman, the film shares similar themes with the novel and copies the relationship between Fanny and Edmund. In the film the characters are transported to the insular upper class debutante society of New York, and the poor Tom escorts the upper class but shy Audrey during the debutante season. Audrey soon falls in love with him. Audrey is an avowed Austen fan in the film, while Tom has read none of the novels and only read literary criticism of Austen. Just like Austen's novel, issues of class and social morality permeate the love story.

🐚 FILMS ABOUT JANE HERSELF 🐚

It's not only Jane's writing that has inspired big screen adaptations – her own life and persona as the author of such beloved romantic tales has produced several films and television series about the lady herself.

BECOMING JANE

This 2007 film stars Anne Hathaway as Jane and tells the story of the writer's love affair with Tom Lefroy, played by James McAvoy. The film is based on the book *Becoming Jane Austen* by Jon Spence, who outlines the relationship (as yet unproven) between Jane and Tom by looking at Jane's letters to her sister Cassandra. The film was criticized for its historical inaccuracies but can be enjoyed as a loose romantic biopic for Austen fans.

THE JANE AUSTEN BOOK CLUB

Based on a novel of the same name, this 2007 film follows the lives of a group of friends who form a book club to read all of Austen's novels. The club is formed of six women (and one man who is roped in as a potential love interest for one of the members). As the members study Austen's novels, they begin to find reflections within their own lives and begin to take on some of the character's traits, such as Emma's match-making and Marianne's extravagant romantic notions.

LOST IN AUSTEN

This ITV four part television series was loosely based on the events of *Pride and Prejudice*, and follows the experience of Amanda Price, a girl from 2008 who discovers Elizabeth Bennet in her bathroom. Amanda goes through the portal Elizabeth came through and finds herself in Longbourn while Elizabeth remains in 21st century London. As Amanda tries to keep the events of the novel on track she inevitably gets in the way and things don't go to plan – for example Jane marries Mr Collins instead of Bingley. Things turn out well though, with Elizabeth staying in modern London as a nanny and Amanda marrying Darcy. There is currently a big screen version of the series in production.

MISS AUSTEN REGRETS

The BBC produced this film in 2008. It stars Olivia Williams as Jane and looks at the last few years of Jane's life as she is inspired to reflect on her own life after her niece Fanny asks for advice on finding a husband. The film was also broadcast in America as part of a series called *The Complete Jane Austen*.

JANE AUSTEN IN MANHATTAN

This 1980 Merchant Ivory production was released in both the UK and the US and tells the story of two rival theater companies that are both bidding for a newly discovered play, written by Austen when she was 12. The film stars Anne Baxter and Robert Powell as the competing directors, and Sean Young in her first ever film role. The story is based on the true tale of LWT, who were interested in producing a play of an Austen manuscript sold at Sotheby's, without ever having seen the manuscript. The manuscript turned out to be too rough to produce a play, but did inspire this film.

Pocket Fact ♆

Austen's works have not only been made into film adaptations; Marvel comics have released graphic novel editions of Pride and Prejudice *and* Sense and Sensibility.

'I cannot speak well enough to be unintelligible': Glossary

Readers of Austen's novels sometimes come across a word or term that leaves them puzzled. What is Mrs Elton talking about when she is boasting of her brother-in-law's 'Barouche-landau'? And what does Austen mean when she describes a person's 'countenance' as 'amiable' or 'handsome'? This section of the book explains some of the Regency terms which litter Austen's novels to help you become a true Austen expert.

Amiable – A person described as amiable is a friendly, easy-going, happy person who is generally considered to be enjoyable company. Jane Austen frequently used the term sarcastically, as we see in *Pride and Prejudice* where Elizabeth mistakenly uses the term several times to describe Wickham.

Annuity – An annuity (much like today) was an amount of money paid out due to the terms of a will or settlement. For many women in Austen's time this was their only means of subsistence after the death of a husband and we see Fanny and John Dashwood's cruel discussion of annuities in *Sense and Sensibility*, when Fanny remarks 'people always live for ever when there is an annuity to be paid them'.

Assembly Room – The Assembly Room was where the local gentry society gathered for balls, public assemblies and other social events. *Northanger Abbey* mentions both the Upper and Lower Assembly Rooms in Bath.

Baronet – A Baronet was (and still is) a hereditary title that meant the bearer had to be called Sir. We meet two baronets in Austen's novels, Sir Thomas Bertram in *Mansfield Park* and Sir Walter Elliot in *Persuasion*.

Barouche-landau – A small carriage with two rows of seats, meaning the passengers faced each other. This type of carriage had a collapsible top which made it very fashionable, hence Mrs Elton's continuous boasting of her brother-in-law's version.

Being out – If a young woman is described as 'being out' it meant that she had reached the age when she could be courted as a wife. Normally a ball was held in honor of a young lady 'coming out'. Young women that were 'out' attended balls and parties and were allowed to converse with young men in the presence of their chaperone. Young women who were not out were meant to dress more demurely and not join in social niceties. The distinction between the two states was somewhat difficult to discern sometimes, as Tom Bertram discusses in *Mansfield Park*.

Chaise – A closed carriage generally used for traveling.

Cotillion – A French dance for four couples which is performed in a square formation.

Countenance – A person's countenance is their general appearance, but the term could also be used to describe their expression, and therefore, their feelings. As we see in *Northanger Abbey* people were often judged by their countenance: 'Catherine recollected herself, blushed deeply, and could say no more. He seemed to be looking in her countenance for that explanation which her lips did not afford.'

Curricle – A curricle was a two-wheeled carriage that was pulled by two horses and which could seat the driver and one passenger. Henry Tilney drives a curricle in *Northanger Abbey*.

Entailment – An entailment was a legal agreement that stated that inherited property could not be broken up, and could only be inherited through the male line. Hence Mr Collins will inherit Longbourn in *Pride and Prejudice* and John Dashwood inherits Norwood in *Sense and Sensibility*. Austen often uses entails as a plot device, normally as a means to create a desperate situation that young women can only save themselves from by making a prudent marriage.

Gig – A gig was a two-wheeled carriage for two people which would have been drawn by one or two horses. Gigs were popular among the young men of the time, and John Thorpe owns one (which he is very proud of!) in *Northanger Abbey*.

Hack – A hack was a rented carriage, although it was scandalous for a young woman to travel in one alone. This makes the 70 mile journey that General Tilney sends Catherine on in a hack post chaise even more cruel, as the narrator comments 'A heroine in a hack post-chaise, is such a blow upon sentiment, as no attempt at grandeur or pathos can withstand.'

Handsome – In Austen's time it wasn't just men who were described as handsome, the term was also used to describe women, buildings, dresses and so on. We see this term in use in the opening of *Emma* when Austen describes her heroine as 'handsome, clever, and rich'.

Marriage articles – The marriage articles which were drawn up before a marriage were a bit like pre-nuptial agreements today. Essentially they were a contract that outlined the distribution of wealth and property in the marriage, and what would happen if the marriage ended. It is the marriage articles for Lydia and Wickham which Darcy negotiates in *Pride and Prejudice*.

Militia – Jane Austen was writing during the French Revolution and Napoleonic war, a time when England was under constant threat of invasion or war. Therefore several militia regiments were established, made up of volunteer soldiers and stationed throughout the country. Unlike the army, where a man had to be of a respected background and have enough fortune to buy his commission, a man from a lower class could enter the militia as an officer. Jane's own brother Henry joined the Oxford militia in 1793 and members of the militia occur frequently in Jane's novels, particularly *Pride and Prejudice* where the officers cause such a stir among the Bennet girls.

Minuet – A French dance for two people.

Parsonage – The parsonage is the house that was given to the local parson as part of his living. This house would sometimes have land attached to it, but often remained the property of the local landowner, as we see in *Mansfield Park* where it is Sir Thomas' choice who to place in the parsonage.

Pelisse – A pelisse was a long, dress-like coat which was often lined with fur. The Jane Austen House Museum in Chawton is in possession of a pelisse which is believed to have been worn by Jane. It is made of silk with a high collar and long sleeves.

Petticoat – Petticoats were worn under a lady's dress and were made of linen, a sturdier material than the dresses of the time. Some petticoats were decorated but most were plain. One of the main purposes of a petticoat was to protect the hem of a lady's dress, as we see Elizabeth trying to do in *Pride and Prejudice*, but failing in Caroline Bingley's eyes who remarks 'I hope you saw her petticoat, six inches deep in mud, I am absolutely certain; and the gown which had been let down to hide it not doing its office.'

Phaeton – An open carriage with four wheels. The word derives from Ovid's *Metamorphoses* where Phaeton, son of the sun god Apollo, cannot control the horses who pull the chariot containing the sun.

Pianoforte – The traditional name for a piano.

Post chaise – A chaise used with rented horses. For long journeys travelers would use their own horses for part of the journey and then continue on using rented horses while their own were taken home.

Postilion – The person who rides and guides the horse that is pulling a carriage.

Public assembly – A public ball that was open to everyone and generally held at the town assembly rooms. We see a public assembly in *Pride and Prejudice*, where Elizabeth meets Darcy for the first time.

Pump room – The Pump Rooms in Bath were where society gathered to 'take the waters', ie drink the thermal spa water. The Pump Rooms were also the place to meet and socialize, and 'promenade' (ie walk around the room) as we see frequently in *Northanger Abbey* when Catherine goes to meet Eleanor Tilney and Isabella Thorpe.

Quadrille – A dance that is performed by four couples in a square formation.

Reticule – A recticule (also sometimes called a 'ridicule') was a Regency purse in which a lady would carry her essentials such as her calling cards, handkerchief, comb, and other toiletries. They came in a variety of colors and fabrics and many had a drawstring close with a long strap that was worn on the wrist. Many ladies made their own reticules.

Spencer – A Spencer was a tighter fitting, waist length coat, which was similar to a gentleman's coat but without the tails.

Traveling post – Hiring a driver (sometimes called a postilion) and horses and chaise for a journey.

Set – A set is the name given to the group of dancers in a dance, as well as to the series of dances they perform.

Stagecoach – A stagecoach was a form of Regency public transport. Those who couldn't afford their own mode of transport, or couldn't catch a lift could ride in a stagecoach, although these were viewed as a lower class of transport. It was frowned upon for a lady to travel alone, especially in a stagecoach and so she would need a chaperone to accompany her. Regency gentlemen would often ride a horse rather than taking a stagecoach. It was also possible to catch a lift on the Royal Mail coach. These journeys were quicker but more expensive than regular stagecoaches. Austen's house in Chawton was next to a main stagecoach route so the noise of the carriage driving past was a regular occurrence.